ELISABETH'S LISTS

Elisabeth's Lists

A FAMILY STORY

LULAH ELLENDER

GRANTA

Granta Publications, 12 Addison Avenue, London W11 4QR

First published in Great Britain by Granta Books, 2018

An essay based on an early draft of this book appeared in *The Junket*

Lines from *The Waste Land* by T. S. Eliot are reprinted by
kind permission of Faber & Faber (UK)

'Separation' from *The Second Four Books of Poems* by W. S. Merwin
is reprinted by kind permission of Bloodaxe Books

Lines from William E. Stafford's 'A Message from the Wanderer'
are reprinted by kind permission of Graywolf Press

A CIP catalogue record for this book is available
from the British Library.

1 3 5 7 9 10 8 6 4 2

ISBN 978 1 78378 383 0
eISBN 978 1 78378 384 7

Typeset in Calluna by Lindsay Nash
Printed and bound by CPI Group (UK) Ltd, Croydon, CR0 4YY

MIX
Paper from
responsible sources
FSC www.fsc.org   FSC® C020471

For Elisabeth and Helen

CONTENTS

ELISABETH'S FAMILY TREE

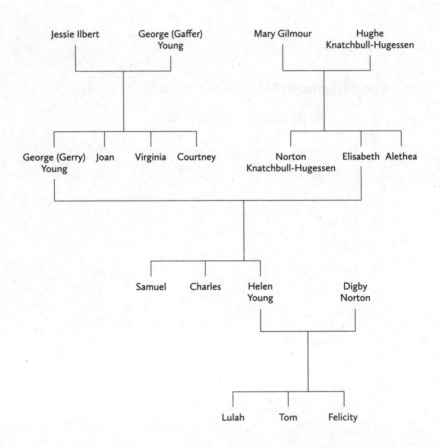

'These fragments I have shored against my ruins'

T. S. Eliot, *The Waste Land*

PROLOGUE

This book grew out of a moment. My mother is standing in her kitchen holding a small red-brown, marbled hardback journal. She tells me that it belonged to her mother, Elisabeth, who died when my mother was just nine years old. She's not sure what to do with it and thinks I might like it. But there is a spark in her eyes. She knows it is no ordinary book; she is giving it to me so that I can find things, dig down into my family's past and show her the treasures I uncover. She is entrusting me with her mother's story. She is handing me a thread and saying, 'Hold this. Follow it. Don't let go. You are going to need it.'

The story of the grandmother I never knew has been passed down through two generations in the sepia photographs, scrawled letters and dramatic anecdotes that constitute a family history. And now, in this book of lists. I have nothing else of Elisabeth's, so it feels immediately precious. Intrigued, I open it and find pages and pages of lists, written between 1939 and 1957, the year she died. From an inventory of household linen to a record of the number of eggs her chickens laid over the course of a year, Elisabeth itemised her days, page after page, and it feels as though I am being offered a glimpse of her life, in fragments and scraps. As I turn the fragile, age-worn pages, I begin to wonder what drove someone to make and keep all these lists.

Making a list is a practice that goes back as far as writing itself. From the Seven Wonders of the World of classical antiquity, through the catalogue of ships in Homer's *Odyssey*, the Ten Commandments in the Bible, the encyclopaedias of the Middle Ages, the eighteenth-century classifications of nature – by the explorer Alexander von Humboldt (who painstakingly recorded geophysical measurements) and the botanist Carl Linnaeus (whose *Systema Naturae* catalogued all known species of plants and animals) – which were part of the Scientific Revolution, on to the horrific death lists of Nazi Germany and right up to today's note-taking apps, we have long jotted down the everyday, the monumental and the necessary.

Whether a throw-away record of tasks ticked off, or an inventory of life-and-death significance, lists give us a par-ticular and peculiar insight into the ways we order and frame our needs. A list provides a purpose and a structure: at its most basic, it can be a guide to how we should use our time; at its most profound, a means to lasso our grief, madness and dreams within neat lines. Lists are an expression of the Hegel-ian notion that we live authentically when we are responsible for creating the order by which we live. These catalogues hold our chaos, they become a bridge between the moment of thought and the moment of action, and make sense of our tumbling ideas. We formulate endless lists of our top films, books or music, of things to do and places to see before we die, as though they might provide both proof of our existence and a legacy for future generations. We believe that a list can make us immortal.

*

A few months after my mother gives me the book of lists, a dress arrives at her house, sent by a distant cousin – a dress that belonged to Elisabeth. It was hand-made by the House of Dior in pale golden silk, and starred with tiny hand-sewn glass beads and pearls, the fabric so diaphanous I am afraid it will disintegrate in my hands. I try it on and it fits perfectly, as if it had been made for me. Something in that moment of climbing into my grandmother's dress makes me feel as if I am stepping into Elisabeth's skin. Enveloped in the fabric that she once wore, it feels as if some part of her is woven into the threads and for the first time I have a sense of her as a person who existed beyond the few stories I grew up with. It felt completely comfortable and otherly all at once.

Until now, Elisabeth's absence has always been a presence, her story spun from the feathered filaments of memories. My mother spoke often of her parents, but there was always a sense of slippage; her memories are hazy and she didn't really know them (if any of us truly know our parents). But I realise that Elisabeth's book of lists might allow me to discover who Elisabeth really was, and to draw out the stories hidden between her beautifully scripted lines.

Elisabeth was born in England in 1915 but spent much of her life overseas. Her father was a diplomat and her short life was characterised by movement and displacement. The book of lists mirrors this constant shifting, with numerous lists for various diplomatic postings and items to be put into storage. I want to trace its movements, to follow its journey from London on the brink of war, to post-Civil War Spain, across the plains of the Middle East, to the mangrove swamps of Brazil and the pomp of Paris, and to the dusty comfort of a stately home.

The book of lists prompts hours of poring over photograph albums, diaries and letters. It leads me to scour country lanes in search of houses Elisabeth once lived in, to read the sad pages of an inquest transcript she never saw and to dig deep into my family's past. Immersed in Elisabeth's world, my own habit of list-making intensifies, and I begin to understand the human impulse to seek order and clarity through the act of writing things down, in neat columns or hastily scribbled lines.

As I embark upon this quest to reconstruct my grandmother's life from the fragments she left behind, I have to decide how much artistic licence I will grant myself. I have used Elisabeth's diaries, letters and of course the lists as carefully as possible, sometimes quoting directly and at other times using the material to feed my imagination. It is important to me that Elisabeth's story is told as faithfully as possible, but I am also acutely aware that this is *my* reading of her, and that other people may have constructed a different version of this same person. Whilst I strive for the truth, I accept that it is *my* truth. There are rabbit holes and dead ends and secrets in this story, and I am balancing fact, imaginings and informed guesswork in order to understand not only my grandmother but my own mother, and myself.

1

China

EVERY TIME I OPEN ELISABETH'S BOOK OF LISTS, I FEEL a childlike sense of delight and anticipation. It has a black cloth spine, a marbled claret-and-black cover and inside the pages are blue-lined with a red double line marking the heading space. Elisabeth writes mostly in black ink, in a small, unfussy hand. Like my mother's. The 'b's and 'y's in particular feel very familiar, the hand movement and pen-strokes passed down to the next generation.

I imagine Elisabeth setting out to buy this journal, in which she would catalogue a new part of her life, turning over different books on the shelf until she found one the right size, the right weight. It reminds me of Augusts as a child, the days before going back to school: I loved choosing school bags and pencils, buying new exercise books and surrounding myself with the reassuring paraphernalia of the stationeryphile. Sometimes we would be in France on holiday and my mother would take us to a *hypermarché* and we would run gleeful-ly up and down the aisles, grabbing tiny pots of glue with little paddles inside the lid, or funny square-lined notebooks from the shelves. These things bring the promise of clarity, preparedness, all the possibilities of the clean page and the emotions we can pour onto it. A fresh term, a fresh start. For Elisabeth with her list book, there was a similar hope that the coming pages would help her navigate a new phase of her life as an adult, and as wife to a man she had first met in China. So, although the book of lists begins its journey in London, it is in Peking (as Beijing was known then) that my search must start.

*

Elisabeth moved to China in 1936, aged twenty-one, when her father took up the post of British ambassador there. China in the 1930s was a place of conflict and contrast, afflicted by floods, famine, political instability and the omnipresent threat of invasion by Japan, and Britain was trying to maintain its grip on the Far East. It was an important posting for Elisabeth's father, and also the furthest posting to which her family had been sent.

The whole family were aware of the turmoil that would surround them, but they had plenty of experience of landing in far-flung places and finding adventure. Elisabeth's father had previously been stationed in Brussels (1921), Paris (1923), Latvia (1930) and Persia (1934), and Elisabeth's early diaries are full of accounts of adventures riding mules up gorges and through gushing torrents, swimming in ice-cold rivers, taking in views of emerald-green rice fields and valleys of flowers, purple skies after rainstorms and landslides, drinking cocoa waiting for the sun to rise over a camp in the mountains, the smells of lilac and wild Judas trees, meeting semi-nomadic

The Forbidden City, 1936

tribespeople, campsites where wolves and panthers prowled after a snowstorm, browsing fine silks in a bazaar, watching a drowned tortoise floating in a sheltered pool, sharing a ship with sixty falcons that are being shipped to the Sheikh of Bahrain.

Elisabeth, her brother, Norton, and her sister, Alethea, had an extraordinary childhood lurching between the thrill of foreign lands and the buttoned-up restrictions of English boarding schools. Norton was two years older, and Alethea three years younger than Elisabeth. The two sisters corresponded regularly throughout their childhood and early adult life. There is a sweet letter written in 1931 by Alethea from Riga, where she is living with her parents, to Elisabeth, who was at boarding school in England. She describes their journey, saying she is 'really an awfully good sailor now' (she was famously sick a lot) and promising that she will send a plan of the room that has been allocated to Elisabeth.

The children knew the challenges of travel, the excitement of new places, the need to fit in amongst strangers. They knew how to spot familiar characters: who would be a friend, who was likely to be trouble, whom they should trust and those they shouldn't. They understood the social mores of diplomatic life and the importance of duty above self. Yet it took its toll on the family, scattered as they were, writing to each other for reassurance and to keep themselves moored. So much of our identity is shaped at a young age by those who surround us, and when the landscape and faces are always shifting it must be difficult to form a definite sense of who we are and where we belong.

Elisabeth's parents were caring but distant: her father, Hughe, was a career diplomat who loved painting and acting, her mother, Mary, a desperately shy woman with a nervous sniff. The few pages of a dictated autobiography Mary began in later life tell of an austere Victorian upbringing, and a cruel governess who told the children they were ugly, stupid and worthless. She recounts how her sister suffered low self-esteem her entire life as a result, and that she herself only became more confident in her thirties. It is no wonder that Mary seems icy and reserved.

Photographs like the one opposite reflect the formal, outward face they presented to the world, and the rigidity of that world. There are only a few pictures of them off guard. One of Elisabeth's father swinging from the mast on a boat gives a glimpse of a playful nature, but, as senior diplomats, they would have been required to conform to strict protocols and complex systems of etiquette.

Elisabeth and her siblings were taught by a governess before being sent to boarding school in England. In the holidays and on foreign postings they were looked after by a nanny, who had been brought up in the slums of the Isle of Dogs and remained with the family (eventually looking after Elisabeth's children) until her death at the age of ninety-seven. She shared her last years with Alethea in a warden-assisted flat, their roles now reversed, Alethea caring for Nanny, but both dependent on each other's friendship. Initially Nanny was known as 'Large', her name being Rosetta (Rose) Large (a wholly inappropriate surname for someone of such diminutive stature), and sometimes as Norris, but later, when I knew her, she was simply

Elisabeth's parents, Mary and Hughe

'Nanny' – her identity awkwardly buried beneath her role. I am reminded of Elisabeth's mother's account of how her own parents did not permit servants to keep their own names – all the footmen were called Andrew and all head housemaids, Jane. But if she minded this loss of individuality, Nanny never mentioned it.

Such a job, in which her own life became so intertwined with those of her employers, required great devotion and sacrifice, and I wonder now if Nanny had any choice. Her work offered her a route out of poverty but at the cost of her own personal life. I know she lost her fiancé in the First World

Rose Large, 'Nanny'

War, and perhaps she never recovered sufficiently to try to meet someone else, preferring to relocate herself in another world. She had great responsibility for her charges, sometimes travelling for weeks across oceans alone with them and unsure exactly where they would stay when they arrived at their destination.

Nanny was unflappable, organised, softly spoken and had a twinkle in her eye behind the round glasses she wore. I remember being shocked when she unravelled her grey hair out of the bun in which it was always pinned, surprised at how long and feminine it was and how she suddenly looked like a different person. She was at once a tidy, well-groomed nanny, and a woman, about whom I knew almost nothing.

Nanny bore no children of her own and devoted her entire working life to Elisabeth's family, raising two generations and being a vital point of stability for children who were constantly uprooted and moved around the globe. She was particularly devoted to Alethea, whose disability after catching polio at the age of eight meant she required more care than the others. When I knew Nanny, she was no longer a servant but truly a member of our family, and greatly loved by us all. She was fond of Rich Tea biscuits, smelt of Pears soap, and would regale us with tales of her adventures in service, like the time in China when she stamped on a tarantula with such force that the paper walls of the house in which they were staying collapsed. My brother once hit her on the head with a toy bus. The pain and shock this caused meant Nanny had to lie down, but after a couple of days feeling very ill and shaken she found that the blow had cured the blindness in one eye from which she had suffered since childhood. A doctor at a London hospital confirmed that miraculously my brother had hit her in exactly the right place to reverse an injury she had sustained around the age of six. So, sometimes, in the roundabout way that happens with children, we did good things for her too. In her later years, Nanny recorded countless stories of her life before and during her time with Elisabeth's family, but I have no idea where these tapes are now.

Her death was the first I can really remember and it seemed unfeasible somehow. We, the third generation of children whose lives she had touched, wanted to scatter crumbs of her favourite Rich Tea biscuits on her coffin, but this was frowned upon. She was our link to the grandparents we never met, a conduit for their stories, and she held a special place in the family. I was surprised when I met her brother at her funeral, so alien was the concept that she had any family or past other than ours. I have her death certificate, which feels oddly intimate and sad.

*

When they first arrive in China, Elisabeth and her family experience few of the problems that flurry outside their small diplomatic sphere. While they wait for a new house to be built in Nanking (the capital city and home to the Chinese Nationalist government of Chiang Kai-shek), they live in the embassy compound in Peking, a city with a dark underbelly, swollen with refugees from the poverty-stricken countryside and Manchuria. In Elisabeth's time, it is a kind of *matryoshka* city – walls within walls, cities within cities, a place of hidden courtyards and forbidden palaces. Camels stride through the city gates at dawn, laden with goods, passing elaborate facades and statuary, marble boats, carved temples and terraced shrines. The streets bustle with pedlars, child barbers shave heads into bowls of water, women sit on the side of the road smoking long pipes and sewing, beside street cafes where people gather to talk and eat. Men take pet birds perched on sticks for walks, fortune tellers provide a constant stream of guidance and direction, a one-man street theatre puts on a puppet show for a keen crowd, children reshape discarded stubs into new cigarettes to sell. And everywhere there is a stench and so much dust that men constantly sprinkle water onto the street using long-handled scoops to try to keep it out of the air. In winter this dust turns to mud so glutinous that one Captain Gordon Casserly wrote of it in 1903: 'never have I gazed on aught to equal the depth, the intensity, and the consistency of the awful mud of Pekin [sic].' An area known as the 'Badlands' is home to poor European expats, opium dens, drug addicts, prostitutes and exiles. Not far away, the Foreign Legation Quarter houses visiting diplomats like Elisabeth's father and his family.

The diplomatic community is surrounded by an imposing – menacing, even – wall, some four metres high, erected around the Legation buildings and manned by armed guards. Chinese inhabitants have been evicted and no Chinese people can enter the Quarter without written permission. Inside the walls are the staff compounds for the various international embassies, as well as hotels, clubs and banks. There are stables, a dairy, a garage, a chapel, tennis courts, barracks, a canteen, a theatre and squash courts. Elisabeth and her fellow residents of the Legation Quarter need never leave, except during the summer, when many of them relocate to the cooler coastal areas (though even there, they live in slightly claustrophobic, cabin-fever-inducing little expat enclaves).

In Peking, the physical separation of the diplomatic staff from the Chinese population causes resentment amongst the local people. There is a perception that the privileged foreigners spend their time holding parties, shopping and going to the theatre. And indeed, the movements of the country-sports-loving diplomatic entourages were determined almost as much by horse races and seasonal fishing spots as by any pressing foreign affairs. In spite of the distinctive local topography and climate, the diplomatic community in Peking recreates a version of the life they have left behind in England (public school, rigid social mores and rules of protocol, a devotion to the notion of 'duty' above individual desires), which means diplomatic families live in a kind of vacuum. They lead a life of privilege and freedom – a life that Elisabeth describes as 'wild and beautiful'.

Occasionally Elisabeth is required for a formal dinner or reception – an accessory to the ambassador, playing her part in representing king and country – but most of the time she lives a fairly aimless existence. Her time is spent riding, playing tennis, learning Chinese and socialising. Elisabeth is much in demand and there are plenty of alcohol-fuelled high jinks. I find a note from Elisabeth and Alethea asking that instead of the waffle-iron they had requested, they should be sent some goldfish bowls, so they could drink brandy from them. One evening Elisabeth and some friends go to the Club for what they imagine will be a quiet evening of Animal Grab and Snap: 'Instead there were crowds of people and after Gerry and Clifford had poured a few sherries down and over us we joined in the free fight for food. Then the riot started: Alethea dropped an entire plate of spaghetti over the floor... Beer was upset in every direction and Franz revealed a strange tendency to throw tomatoes at everyone...We tore home, heaved up the carpets, threw a record on the gramophone, yelled for some whisky and waltzed madly for a bit. Suddenly we were all in the APC mess playing golf with glasses and playing ball with bottles and breaking records on each other's heads and sliding on the floor.'

There are many evenings like this, mostly fun, but sometimes Elisabeth feels exhausted by the pace of it, by the crack and flake of the days, furiously fast yet ending with a peeling emptiness. After manically fizzing with all the frivolity, she suddenly finds herself crashing down when the apparent meaninglessness of her life hits her full square. There is a bad moment when, at a dinner with friends, she feels like screaming the whole evening. She gulps down a mouthful of champagne with the backwash of a sense of terror, clinging on to the table edge as if it is the only real thing in the room and she must not let go or she will disappear. Some days her world is blanketed in a crepuscular shroud, people and objects are dim and far away and she feels as if she is standing alone in a vast, empty expanse. Sometimes she just wants to go home.

Alethea also feels the pressure of having to keep up with the social whirl. I find a note in Elisabeth's diary beside an entry in which Elisabeth expresses concern at the amount of alcohol her sister is consuming, and her worries that Alethea is out of control. The note, written years later in Alethea's fragile, spindly hand and fastened with an incongruously modern orange paper clip, explains how she felt she couldn't sparkle without a drink and how much she lived in the shadow of her older sister's vivaciousness and intelligence. Alethea also adds, apologetically, that the seemingly inde-cent amounts of champagne sloshing around the Legation were in fact cheap local bottles of fizz. As an elderly woman, living alone in her sheltered flat in Oxford, with its corridors carpeted in lurid green, a shaky lift, the view of a church spire and pleasant garden, Alethea used Elisabeth's diaries

Alethea

to transport herself back to that golden past, re-immersing herself in that eddying, lilting, tainted time. It was Alethea who kept Elisabeth's book of lists for all those years, packed away with the diaries and fading photographs.

Although the British officially move the embassy to Nanking in September 1936, Elisabeth and her family divide their time between Nanking and Peking. Among the diplomatic residents in Peking there is a growing general awareness of the menace Japan poses to China – sporadic outbreaks of fighting have occurred since the Japanese invasion of Manchuria in 1931 – but those inside the Legation remain largely unaffected by the poverty and wider political problems facing the country, until a brutal murder exposes a seam of violence beneath their relatively carefree existence.

In January 1937, a nineteen-year-old girl named Pamela Werner, the adopted daughter of a retired British consul, is found dead on the edges of the Badlands, beneath a watchtower said to be haunted by fox spirits. She had been disfigured and her internal organs removed, her heart ripped from her chest. The murder is front-page news and Elisabeth and her friends must have been disturbed by the death, particularly as the girl was of a similar background and age to them, although there is no mention of the event in Elisabeth's diaries, possibly because she moved to Nanking soon after the murder. The culprit is never found, but the investigation exposes a seedy underworld of drugs, sex parties and foreigners involved in rapes and predatory attacks on young women. The case is put aside, and there have since been accusations of a cover-up by the British consulate to protect people from within the Legation who may have been involved. It leaves a sense of unease and fear, and, just a few weeks later, danger strikes closer to home.

*

It is 2 February 1937. A biting wind blows down from the Siberian plains across the wooded Purple Mountains outside Nanking, but the afternoon is bright and clear. Elisabeth is out riding with friends. Her horse is skittish but she is happy, heading for home and enjoying the sight of water buffalo grazing in the paddy fields through the hoof-whipped dust. Suddenly, a shot cracks the air. She hears a whizzing sound and feels a forceful blow to her forehead.

Terrified, she reaches a hand to her head, fearing it has been half blown off. She finds it intact but pouring with blood. 'I've been hit! A bullet!' she cries, hurling herself to the ground. The bullet entered above her left eye and skimmed across her forehead. Now, cool and still, it is lodged in the thin bone. One of her party, a young diplomat named Gerry Young, leaps from his horse and searches frantically for something he can use to remove the bullet. He finds a long, thin door key in his pocket and uses it to prod gently at the bleeding wound, eventually managing to gouge the bullet from her head.

*

This attack is the first time Elisabeth is directly affected by the surrounding violence in China, and it must have been terrifying. It is still unclear whether her party was a specific target or whether Elisabeth was caught in the cross-fire between warring bandits; there are even suggestions that the gun was a rook rifle fired by a Chinese sportsman. But what really captures people's attention is the ingenious rescue by the young diplomat, Gerry, and news of the shooting spreads. The British press get hold of the story and, as Elisabeth recounts, they report the incident with a charming and wholly inaccurate flourish: 'Gerry, so the story goes, spurred forward in knightly fashion and swinging the chancery keys on their chain like a mace, felled the assailant before he could reload his blunderbuss.'

This is how I have always seen Gerry: the quick-thinking, dashing hero, struck with sudden love for the injured woman swooning in his arms. The shooting has become woven into our family folklore, an impossibly romantic rescue that sowed the seeds of future love. In reality, the incident seems to have little immediate effect on either Gerry or Elisabeth (there was no noticeable scar left by the bullet), apart from the fact that Gerry now makes sure he always carries tweezers in his pocket when out riding. But the shooting does cause an imperceptible shift in their friendship, an unspoken debt and recognition that something extraordinary has passed between them. It may also have had a longer-term effect on Elisabeth's nerves and her sense of the fragility of life.

In the following weeks, the increasingly war-like hostilities between Japan and China begin to cause concern amongst the inhabitants of the Legation Quarter, and many leave for Nanking or Shanghai. While Elisabeth's father remains in Peking to continue his diplomatic duties, she,

Norton, Alethea and their mother are sent to Pei-tai-ho in the countryside, where they exist in a kind of peaceful limbo, unsure whether they will be evacuated to England or to Japan, as China descends into chaos. Elisabeth enjoys this time in the rural hinterlands, and describes her surroundings in this diary extract:

> The sandy road, green fields stretching away to the mountains. In the village were groups of Chinese babies – no clothes except for absurd scarlet aprons, their hair cut in fantastic patterns on their heads, they eat peaches and dirt indiscriminately amongst the donkeys…Hawkers were wandering along the shady path at the edge of the road, bundles of silk and linens on their backs…I found Alice [a British diplomatic wife] sitting with accounts on her verandah: her servants know very little English, and she was wondering why she'd been charged for 'I winnowing-fan' and 'to stuffing one bat 40 cents'.

Elisabeth's gentle life of bicycling, sleeping, reading and eating is interrupted in July 1937 when a Japanese fighter plane attacks her father's car on a journey from Nanking to Shanghai. The car is strafed by machine-gun fire, and then bombed as the party tries to escape. The bomb blows the driver into the air before knocking him temporarily unconscious, and Elisabeth's father is seriously injured. He said later that for the first fifteen minutes after the attack he was completely paralysed and didn't think he could possibly live. But they somehow manage to drive fifty miles to safety in Shanghai. News of the attack reaches Elisabeth via a patchy wireless report from which she can only make out the words 'not dangerously'. She rushes to the other diplomats' houses to gather more information, the rickshaw slipping and floundering on mud-pool paths washed away by rain. News drips in excruciatingly slowly, but they eventually formulate a plan: her mother is to be dispatched by warship to Shanghai, where her father is being treated. They hurriedly pack, her mother flinging clothes into a suitcase, while Elisabeth lights a cigarette, the hot dry smoke replacing the panic that is congealing in her throat.

After another difficult journey down to the seashore and a rushed goodbye, Elisabeth waits anxiously on the beach, her torch following the path of the speedboat carrying her mother into the darkness, towards the hulking ship. Soon the slapping wake leaves the light behind and her mother has disappeared. Left to await orders about what to do next, Elisabeth stays in the village. She has to endure a lunch party with a Japanese man, which causes great awkwardness on both sides, not helped by his comment that he must leave because his aircraft is needed to go and bomb Nanking.

A cholera outbreak threatens to stall Elisabeth's attempts to visit her father, but there is a flurry of planning and finally she sets off for Shanghai. She travels in a warship, the heft of the vessel bolstering her spirits, yet as the ship leaves the harbour she is uneasy about the demolished villages, shipwrecks and smouldering buildings they pass.

The British Government are shocked by the attack on the ambassador, which some denounce as tantamount to an attack on the king, but they are unwilling to alienate Japan further. The official Japanese explanation is that the pilot mistook the diplomatic party for a Chinese official they were targeting. The British demand an apology but no retaliatory action is taken. Elisabeth's father is awarded a sum in compensation, and makes a slow recovery. In December 1937 it is decided he should return to England, after touring Indonesia and Singapore *en route*. At 2 a.m. one morning the family receive the news that they are to be sent home with him, their time in China coming to an abrupt end. They are overjoyed: 'The whole family was awake so we all went mad all over the house & squealed with joy. We sail in under a week, & London in 5 weeks. Incredible. Excitement and fleas kept me awake most of the night.'

2

Eaton Place, London

Wedding - Presents.

Date	From.	Present	Answered.
Dec. 7ᵗ	Mrs. Fisher-Rowe, 49 Thurloe Sq.	Table cloth	Dec. 8
" 8ᵉ	Miss Legh, 75 Eaton Square	Glass Jug	Dec. 9ᵉ
" 10	Mr. & Mrs. Loch	7 greenish champagne	
" 14ᵉ	~~Lady B~~	glasses	Dec. 10ᵉ
" 14ᵉ	Lady Brabourne	cheque : £25	Dec. 14ᵉ
" 14ᵉ	Jock & Sue Leward	Watch ring	Dec. 14ᵉ
" 16ᵉ	Lady Constance Milnes Gaskell	3 Bath towels, etc.	Dec. 18ᵉ
" 19	Barbara Lindsay, 7 Audley Square	Fire guard	Dec. 19ᵉ
" 22	Betty Loyd	£10:10	Dec. 22ⁿᵈ
Dec. ?	Sir Orme Sargent	Wooden Tray	Jan. 9ᵉ
Jan. 7ᵉ	Nanny	Sewing machine	—
Jan. 8ᵉ	Lady Nan Bevan	Book: Rembrandt	Jan. 9ᵉ
16ᵉ	Grandpapa	Pearl necklace	9ᵉ
11ᵉ	Granny	Aquamarine ring	12ᵉ
12	Cousins Molly & Doreen	Picnic basket	15ᵉ
13	Elizabeth	Sheep skin rug	13
15ᵉ	Lady Sligo	China tray & six pots	15ᵉ
15ᵉ	Aunt Margaret A.	Brooch	15
	Akethei	Dressing - table etc. etc.	—
16ᵉ	Hopes Jun.	Triple Mirror	18

For all the excitement about coming back to England, this return is not an easy one for Elisabeth, now aged twenty-three. It is a homecoming, but they have no home. In January 1938, she and her family arrive by train at Victoria Station in London after their long voyage. They are met by photographers, reporters and relatives; policemen are holding back the crowd that has gathered to see the wounded ambassador. Walking to the waiting car, Elisabeth inhales the familiar stale-sweet London air, with its tang of metal dust and bread and coal smoke. She hears a woodpigeon's soft call, the sound of a train rattling past and a wireless somewhere playing music. China already seems like a lifetime ago. She sinks her chin into her fur collar and flops down onto the leather seat in the waiting car, next to her mother.

As they pull away from the station Elisabeth is shocked to see muddy gashes where trenches are being dug in the elegant squares and parks, people queuing for gas masks, tube stations closed for urgent alterations, propaganda posters flapping from lamp posts and the hollow husks of evacuated hospitals. These images flash past, creating a surreal montage of a country bracing itself for war. London, while still beautiful and full of life, is entering a dark time. In the dim streets, there are violent demonstrations against Oswald Mosley's British Union of Fascists, exposing racial tensions and the plight of Jewish refugees fleeing the Nazis in Europe.

The family take up residence in London in a rented house in Eaton Place, a grand road in Belgravia, with creamy, reassuringly solid Regency buildings. They begin to unpack the few belongings they have brought with them, adjusting and rearranging the furniture as they must rearrange their vision of this new life in London. Elisabeth takes an instant dislike to the 'dark, dank house', which is full of other people's 'china and knick-knacks, and what the inventory men call "whatnots". The inventory men kept on buzzing around making lists whilst I was writing letters & I found it hard not to write "One pr. of slightly soiled bellows, carved cupid handles" etc etc. Anyhow, here we are, for better or for worse.' There must have been something eerie about these houses filled with the belongings of strangers, with the shadows and imprints of previous families, and with the sense that you too are merely temporary residents whom the house will shrug off when your replacements arrive.

During these first weeks back in London, Elisabeth feels miserable. She is also resentful of the role she has to play as an ancillary member of the diplomatic service. There is a petulant outburst in her diary, balking at the tasks frequently delegated to her by her mother: 'I object to being used as a kind of secretary, and made to do all the telephone calls Mother can't be bothered to. I HATE it. I hate the cramping atmosphere of the family in London…I hate everyone, and they think I'm intolerable. What's more, I don't give two hoots.' She is in a halfway place, still a dependent but ready to strike out on her own. In spite of her tetchiness, Elisabeth is aware that the move has been difficult for her family too, noting that 'Mother seems care-worn and displeased. Hope she will enjoy herself a bit.' Unfortunately, there is not much chance for her mother to enjoy herself. She is concerned about where they might be posted during what looks like an inevitable international conflict – and also has worries about money. The compensation Elisabeth's father was promised after the Japanese strafing never materialised, and the family have standards to maintain, a 'face' to present. Norton seems rather absent from Elisabeth's life at this time but she mentions him being 'busy with his book, which he says produces more ideas and material as he proceeds!'. There is no record of this book, no lost manuscript for me to uncover, but I have often imagined its contents: something historical, factual, based on a faraway place.

London retains its elegance and bustle – people still shop in well-stocked department stores, they stroll in the parks – but smog envelops the dingy squares and dark alleys, like the blanket of anxiety that wraps itself quietly around the city's inhabitants. Elisabeth finds London 'blank and depressing' and visits different parts of the country whenever she can, taking refuge with friends. She is happiest when staying at her cousin's house, Parham, in Sussex, where she is woken at 10 a.m. with hot-house peaches and the newspaper.

When she is in London, Elisabeth's life is punctuated by glamorous social events, like a visit to Buckingham Palace for the Derby Day ball. Elisabeth enjoys getting dressed for these occasions: the long soak in the bath, the spritz of cologne, the dusting of powder and slick of lipstick. One night, she watches, star-struck, as the king and queen dance a sheepish foxtrot, whilst a platinum-blonde crooner's vampish voice echoes around the duchesses and ambassadresses, and rebounds down miles of corridors and picture galleries. She frequents clubs like the Gargoyle (popular with a bohemian clientele) and the Florida (favourite of the society set), often

Elisabeth in London

dancing until 5 a.m. She drinks with her old friend Betty Sackville-West, whom she describes as a 'queer person. From being absolutely wild she switches suddenly to a posture of almost dowager-like dignity'. She plays cards with a duke and a duchess who carried Queen Mary's train at the coronation. She waltzes on revolving floors and 'wobbles' around town in search of fun. Yet, 'everything feels as if it were crumbling, declining...decaying'.

After one night out dancing, Elisabeth takes a taxi home with a male friend, who makes an unwelcome advance during the journey. Elisabeth is shaken up and notes the event in her diary with an almost tangible shiver. This kind of ambush was not uncommon. When young debutantes were launched into society for the season they were frequently accompanied home by men they didn't know well, and by the 1950s they had developed a code to enable them to identify the ones to avoid: NSIT (Not Safe in Taxis); MTF (Must Touch Flesh); VVSITPQ (Very Very Safe in Taxis Probably Queer).

When she gets back to Eaton Place after these lively nights, Elisabeth feels an old sense of unsettling dread. It is unsurprising, she reassures herself – the country is in the midst of preparations for war. She is deeply troubled by Hitler's aggression and fears the horrors to come. The family's clothes have gone missing in transit on the return voyage and Elisabeth is also adrift, bobbing on a viscous tide of inertia, struggling to find a sense of purpose in London. She misses her life in China.

From the distance of London, she is largely able to overlook the fact that she didn't have anything important or meaningful to do there either. What are the things that call her back? Is it the otherworldliness of food like duck's tongue, or the markets selling exquisite silks, or the exhilaration of swimming in a typhoon-tossed sea, sucked by the current and tumbled by the surf? Or the rousing dangers of a broiling war, darting across a foreign city with a soldier, watching a plane drop a bomb on a station, shrapnel falling around her and melting into the charred remains of buildings? Elisabeth has become accustomed to the perpetual sensual barrage of China: the sights, the smells, the mental readjustments that she believes make it easier to stay alive. Perhaps it is the fact that just by existing within that frenzied, bohemian, luminous world she could mostly keep herself from examining the darkness she holds in her head. Coming home with no job, no place at university and no husband, Elisabeth comes undone.

She knows that she 'ought' to be feeling happy to be back but she is, in fact, lost and desperate. She confesses in her diary that she can see only 'utter blank depression everywhere, in spite of the sun. It feels like the blackest day imaginable. There seems not a sliver of hope.' This is not the first time she has felt low. I find references in her diaries to life being 'hell', she speaks of 'general beastliness' and feeling 'beastly and unsettled'. In December 1937, on the long sea voyage back from China, she writes: 'One ruminates a lot at sea. It's funny how one's mood affects everything – how some days the most trivial jobs seem worthwhile, and others the whole of life seems pointless. One could live more fully if one's moods were under control…happiness is far from one's grasp when every whim & temper can get the upper hand.'

She also describes times of feeling unbearably restless, her mind in turmoil, of being violently antisocial and staying in bed for two days of depression.

Now, back in London, she tries to find a way out of the slump: 'Can't fit in half of the things I want to...But if I read on my own I hope to accomplish something, and also avoid that awful "hectic" feeling which is so fatal.' I think back to those descriptions of life in China, the whirl and frenzy, Elisabeth lining up rows of people on the floor and leaping over them again and again, unable to contain her energy, and wonder what a modern-day doctor would have made of her behaviour.

There are places in her diaries where she tries to talk herself round, as if by stating her determination to 'not be selfish' and to control her emotions she is more likely to succeed. My mother thinks Elisabeth was seeing a psychiatrist during this period in London, but I can't find any reference to this other than when she mentions that 'psycho-analyses & reports on results are a bit of a strain'. She often feels angry at herself for not being stronger, for not feeling happy or grateful. I wish she could have read Camus' words: 'It is not humiliating to be unhappy. Physical suffering is sometimes humiliating, but the suffering of being cannot be, it is life.'

Eventually, by the middle of 1938, Elisabeth begins to settle. She takes a cookery class (where the instructor talks about 'what I call the *salt*...and what I always call *soup*'), learns dressmaking (as expected of a woman), and finds a role in a French play that serves as the perfect distraction from her sadness. She takes a job at Great Ormond Street hospital working as an occupational therapist. She is taught carpentry and the basics of psychiatry, which she loves and describes as 'enormous fun'. There is a symbiotic rebuilding going on here – she is patiently helping others to construct things out of wood, as she builds herself a life. Some trunks finally arrive from China, and she begins to unpack things she hasn't seen since Nanking, memories folded into each garment. Like the sediment that sinks to the bottom of a river, her worries recede. Elisabeth describes this settling as 'stabilising myself', as if it is a skill she has learned through all her moves around the world. An initial wild, sad period followed by a more steady life. Although, while she is still dependent upon her parents, it is a life that can at any moment be uprooted at the whim of the Foreign Office.

*

Meanwhile, Gerry is still in China, and hating every moment of it. The British diplomats are forced to follow the Chinese government from city to city as each place becomes too dangerous. The embassy has retreated from the fighting to Shanghai, and Gerry is one of the few left there. He joined the Foreign Office in 1931 and was posted to Peking in 1935 after an initial posting in Berlin. From various sources, I gather pieces of information about him: he is a clever, witty man, a keen linguist, who loves doing *The Times* crossword, reading P. G. Wodehouse and composing limericks (I find an extraordinary set of Nazi propaganda postcards with photographs of Hitler in various dramatic poses, and on the back of each Gerry has composed a limerick satirising the German leader in his contorted stances). He is also a good dancer, well turned-out, a dangerously fast driver and is keen on boats – his favourite sailing knot is a round-turn and two half-hitches. His face is a charmingly handsome mixture of dimples, wonky nose, quizzical eyebrows and a full mouth that was usually pursed into a smile.

When Elisabeth and Gerry first met, Elisabeth actually disliked him, describing him as 'small and rather shaky', and she was unsettled by his rather out-of-control drinking and the frequent reprimands he received for his bad behaviour. Her father liked working with him, but described him as 'weak as a kitten'. Gerry and Elisabeth quickly became close friends, however, and had fun together, waltzing on rooftops and riding in the hills.

Now, while Elisabeth is safely back in London, Gerry is stuck in the middle of the brutal Sino-Japanese conflict in an embassy from which most people have been evacuated. He begins to write letters to Elisabeth. He is bored and suffering from a combination of jealousy at imagining her dancing with other men in London, a stifling heatwave and an unspecified stomach problem. When he eventually hears that he is to be sent home, he begins a letter to Elisabeth at his desk: 'Only three more days in this cess-pit...' His office is across the road from a dentist, from where, he says, 'there passes a constant stream of groaning, yelling, cursing wretches. Sometimes a pretty girl turns up but no girl looks her best when practically all you can see is her tonsils. What with the heat, the screams of pigs and the dentists' patients, I will be quite at home when I arrive in Hell.'

It is a strange courtship: initially the tone of the letters is humorous and affectionate, but Elisabeth also has other suitors and is in love with another young diplomat named Paul. This was unlikely ever to come to anything, as Paul was one of the few men who crossed Elisabeth's path not to fall in love with her. I search for a picture of him online and note his remarkably hairy eyebrows with a hint of relief that that particular attribute did not enter my family gene pool. Gerry is single, but I am not sure at first whether he is writing solely to Elisabeth, or whether he is wooing other eligible young women, as he hints in his letters at the effectiveness of writing poetry for women to whom he has taken a fancy. Previously he had a serious relationship in Berlin with a glamorous Russian woman, but this ended sadly and mysteriously. It soon becomes clear, however, that he has fallen for Elisabeth.

He writes to her regularly, using his customary Parker 51. The pen is weighty and smooth, and his words glide onto the page, beginning timorously, but gradually becoming less hesitant, as he grows sure of his feelings through the act of writing them down. The letters reveal his growing frustration that she is so far away, and finally, in one of his last letters before leaving China, he refers to 'love': 'This is more by way of love than a letter, though more passion and a little less about the behaviour of my stomach would be indicated.' Humour deflects and neutralises the sentiment, yet the word 'love' remains, tucked quietly into a sentence, but radiating nonetheless. There is a sense of urgency about his letters now: he must get back before Elisabeth marries someone else (his brother, he feared), or her father moves them all somewhere obscure and inaccessible and she is lost for ever. Had their story been a Hollywood movie, their love would have been apparent the moment Gerry extracted the bullet from Elisabeth's head. In fact it is revealed incrementally, a gentle peeling back of expectations and preconceptions to reveal the simple truth that Gerry wants her to be his wife.

His relief at being ordered to return home is ineffable. The Trans-Siberian Express plucks Gerry from his hellhole in the autumn of 1938 and winds its slow way across the relentless landscape, passing through vast barren plains, past ice floes and distant peaks. Gerry amuses himself on the long journey by composing poems. He sends the one overleaf to Elisabeth, with a note stating that it is the first and only poem she will receive from Omsk.

He quips that he is fondly cherishing the memory of a lovely girl, and will arrive to find a shrivelled and toothless hag, making a joke out of the fear inherent in long-distance love that the other person will have changed or will not hold the same magic when we are reunited. Despite these apprehensions, as soon as he arrives back in London in October he goes straight to a party to find her.

Elisabeth recounts their meeting at the party in her diary: 'I caught a glimpse of Gerry's face at the other side of the room. I dashed towards it, knocking people over right and left. It seemed amazing and thrilling to see him again…It's funny not meeting for nearly 18 months to find people nicer than ever. I danced with Gerry and he asked me to marry him. That, I admit, rather dumbfounded me…' She obviously not only still has teeth, but is as lovely as he remembered.

Intourist USSR

ABOARD THE
TRANS-SIBERIAN
EXPRESS
SHORTEST ROUTE BETWEEN
EUROPE AND THE FAR EAST

Wiedersehen.

I wonder what you'll think of me, + what I'll think of you.
For eighteen months can do a lot. And gosh it's done it too
As far as I'm concerned at least. I've put on forty pounds,
My hair is grey, my eyes are pink, my chins have broken bounds;
I've quite forgotten all the things that once you thought were funny
And all I ever talk about is Chiang Kai-shek, or Money.
And so you'll understand how very worried I must be
As here I sadly sit + think what you will think of me.

I wonder what I'll think of you, + what you'll think of me.
Will the You Ive always dreamt of be the You that I shall see?
Or have you dyed your lovely hair? Or have you learnt to flirt +
Or have you told Li-Lan to say that if I call you're out?
Or do you love a Russian Blue, a Siamese, or a Wop?
Have you gone all Oxford Groupy? Do you call your Father 'Pop'?
Oh dear oh dear oh dear oh dear, I shan't know what to do.
If, after all, you're different from what I think is You.

— Omsk. 8. xi. 38

(And I bet this is the only poem you ever
have got , +probably ever will get,
from Omsk)

Poem written on the Trans-Siberian Express

Elisabeth doesn't give Gerry a response to his proposal straight away. They spend the evening catching up and as she slides into a taxi her head is spinning from the drink and Gerry's sudden declaration. She doubts her ability to make such a momentous decision. What if they have nothing more in common than China? What if she hates married life? Does she really want to be a diplomat's wife, after all these years of uprooting? Does she really love him? She sleeps fitfully, throwing these thoughts around. In the morning, when she gets to work at the hospital there is a telephone call for her. It's Gerry. He asks her again to marry him. She hesitates and writes him a letter later that day: 'You can't imagine what a curious crowd there was in the room when you rung up this morning: one nervous breakdown (modelling a polar bear), one decaying gentleman who was hammering on some wood very loudly, and one instructress...' She writes again that evening: 'Tonight. Just before going to sleep. Yes, I am drawn towards the idea of marrying you. Forsooth a capital plan. Darling Gerry, it will be so perfect. I know it will, and I've never known anything was perfect before – tra, tra-la-di-diddle.'

Her acceptance is hedged in humour, as though she cannot quite acknowledge the seriousness of the commitment she is making, but privately, the fuzziness of her doubts is already being replaced by a surety that marriage is a good idea. Elisabeth begins imagining a wedding and their first home together, the furniture and objects that would transpire as gifts later, the things she would log and store and use for years to come.

Gerry and Elisabeth become officially engaged on 23 November 1938, and their wedding date is set for just three months' time – it will be a short engagement to fit in with her father's imminent new posting to Turkey. With the announcement, the couple's affections are freed up and they allow themselves to dive into their relationship. Like the inosculation of tree branches they begin to grow together, melting into each other. On a weekend visit to a mutual friend they are separated by the long halls of the country house and send each other love notes. In one, Elisabeth writes: 'DARLING, DARLING, DARLING, I'm just going to get up. I'm longing to kiss you good morning, so get out of your bath sometime before lunch. Every scrap and atom of my love, angel.' In another, Gerry writes, with customary wit and seemingly fuelled by a large amount of alcohol, 'Adio Tesoro mio. Remember it was always you. Or nearly always.'

I also find an intriguing note folded like an arrow, addressed to Elisabeth in Gerry's hand. I am reluctant to unfold it in case I can't put it back, but I am too curious, and the creases are so deep that it falls easily into place. Inside the note is this rather cryptic message, which I think may refer to the first time they slept together: 'Any concern for me to worry about this morning? I am sorry you're going.' It was written before they were married, which might explain the folding, the diplomat schooled in cyphering and encryption protecting his lover's dignity by folding his question into this puzzle. I am aware that there is a parallel here, too, with my unfolding of Elisabeth's book of lists: I must treat it carefully, gently, respecting the creases whilst also exposing the contents. I am afraid that once opened, I may never be able to get it back how it was. That *I* may never be how I was.

In the lead-up to their marriage, there are flickers of nerves and worries that the other person will stop loving them once their flaws are known. They both experience the anxiety that often lurks beneath the surface of burgeoning love – that we are inherently unlovable, and that once someone really gets under our skin they will begin to despise us. In truth, falling in love requires a fluttering mutual suspension of disbelief, to overlook things we may not find appealing.

As Alain de Botton writes: 'Is there not in every *coup de foudre* a certain wilful exaggeration of the qualities of the beloved, an exaggeration that distracts us from disillusion by focusing our energies on a given face, in which we are briefly and miraculously to believe?' Indeed, this distraction must dissolve into acceptance of another's foibles, for this is where real love happens. According to Anaïs Nin, 'Where the myth fails, human love begins. Then we love a human being,

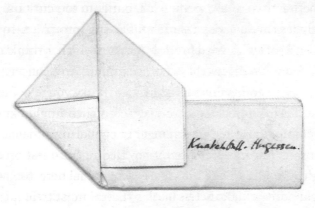

Folded note from Gerry

not our dream, a human being with flaws.' As a relationship develops, we must exist on both hope and understanding.

And we may turn to lists. We make accounts of what we love about a person, like the architect Eero Saarinen's list of his beloved wife's good points ('clever, hansome [sic], perceptive, generous, marvelous sense of humor'), so that we can somehow write these things into being. We may set out the imagined shape of our relationship, like Einstein's brutal list of Conditions for Marriage, written to his wife as their marriage crumbled ('You will renounce all personal relations with me…You will not expect any intimacy from me…you will stop talking if I request it'). Charles Darwin also used a list to work through whether or not he wanted to be married. His pros and cons of marriage set out his thoughts on the tensions between the stability and companionship of a marriage, and the restrictions such a relationship would impose upon his work and travel. In one remarkably unromantic entry under the 'Marry' heading, he notes that a wife would be 'better than a dog anyhow'. Thanks to the list, Darwin concludes that marriage is preferable, imagining 'a nice soft wife on a sofa with good fire, & books & music perhaps'. I only hope Emma Wedgewood, who became his wife six months later, never saw his premarital deliberations.

I am sure Elisabeth and Gerry go through a similar process of weighing up whether or not to marry during their short courtship. And once decided, they plunge fully and squarely into the idea. They are clearly a good match, and other people notice this too. Elisabeth's father includes in a letter a comment from an aunt: 'I had Elisabeth and Gerry over for the afternoon. Two happier people I have never seen. They do not seem to have a thought apart, and are so pleased with everything.'

*

The wedding presents start arriving in December 1938. Gifts continue to be sent until May the following year, meaning months of recording and thanking. This is the first time in Elisabeth's life that she has been fully responsible for ordering the detail of her domestic life. And so she buys a book in which to keep track of it all.

The first, and longest, entry in what becomes her book of lists is a list of wedding presents. It is here that we begin, amidst the tablecloths and wooden trays, her hopes and anxieties whorling invisibly amongst the carefully inked lines. Over sixteen pages she has logged all the presents given to her and Gerry on the occasion of their marriage, as well as the names of the present-givers, and the date of her thank-you reply. Opposite the first page is a child's sticky-fist scribble in pencil, an anachronistic jump forward to the children she and Gerry will have. The variation in the thickness of the ink on this first page gives the list the feeling of a tidal flow: dark to light, heavy to faint. It seems to mirror the energy it took to write such a long catalogue of gifts, the change in mood from day to day, the waxing and waning of resolve. There is a small blue ink stain at the bottom of the page, which is startling amongst the monochrome of the photographs and letters I have been immersed in. Rebecca Solnit writes, 'The world is blue at its edges and in its depths' and to me, the blueness in

Elisabeth's book is a reminder of something more – of the future – and a smudgy footnote of hope. This blue reaches beyond the book of lists; it is the bruised blue of sky reflected in the river that winds past Elisabeth's last, and only, real home. It is the viridian blue of my mother's eyes.

As I turn these first pages, I wonder how Elisabeth felt about each of these presents. Most of the gifts are for the couple's new house, but there are also some personal items such as jewellery, books and bags, as well as money. The Turkish ambassador sent orchids, a refreshingly colourful gift amongst the stuffier household objects. Although some of the presents seem rather miserly (cocktail sticks, a mustard pot, 'old' china ornaments), the list reads like an inventory of an upper-middle-class house, with its silver muffin tin, numerous vases and art books. The names of the guests and present-givers also reflect the grandness of the couple's social circle: a viscount, a duchess, a baroness, several ladies at the court of Queen Mary, senior diplomats, a shipping magnate and numerous lords and ladies.

I imagine Elisabeth sitting in her bed in Eaton Place wearing her orange Chinese-silk pyjamas, eating breakfast from one of the selection of trays laid with one of the six (*six!*) early morning tea sets they have been given, writing her lists. As the sounds of London thrum beyond her window, she strokes the sapphire stone of her engagement ring. Her fingers are long, with a prominent knuckle – they are fingers that I recognise, family resemblances, like the whip of hair at her forehead and her high cheekbones. She wears her brown hair in the pre-war fashion, just above the shoulders with curls around the edges. She is quietly beautiful: composed yet sparkly, with a wavy smile that creases the skin around her eyes.

Placing the tea tray on the bed beside her, she reaches for the new journal she has bought and opens the cover. She smooths the first page flat and writes a heading: WEDDING PRESENTS. She notes the latest gift (a triple mirror) and composes a reply in her head, and as the presents accrue, so does the reality of the new life she is embarking upon. In her small black diary she checks that appointments have been made for the day before the wedding: 'Feet 12, Hair & Face 3'. She will be ready. It is a time of great hope for her, but there is fear here too – her personal happiness is set beneath the unsettling penumbra of a country sliding into war. A strange time to be married, the last Valentine's Day before the world would be changed for ever.

*

When Elisabeth and Gerry are married two families are also united. The wedding-present list reveals the privileged world both came from, but they grew up in families that were quite different in disposition.

Elisabeth's parents were conservative and respectable, with a strong Christian faith and a belief in duty and tradition. Their marriage appears to have been a happy one, with Elisabeth's mother supporting her husband in his diplomatic roles. Elisabeth's father was a slim man with a neat moustache and a round face capped with a thin slick of hair. His small features were precise and he was well turned out; he is often in the background of photographs, watching from the sidelines. Elisabeth's mother had the kind of glacial beauty that women in her position often display. Her cheekbones bloomed with a flush that revealed her shyness, and her downward-sloping curl of a mouth rarely broke into a smile. When she attended functions, she performed her role perfectly efficiently, but was acting out of love for her husband rather than enjoyment.

Amongst the boxes of family papers my mother has given me, I discover three soft, flimsy envelopes, full of correspondence between Elisabeth's parents in the years 1938 and 1948. As I read I am struck by how affectionately they write to each other, but also of the great disconnect in their marriage caused by working for the Foreign Office. Their letters often express their sadness during the times they are kept apart by international conferences or travel requirements, and they seem to live quite separate lives from their grown-up children.

Gerry's family was strikingly different. His father, Sir George Young (known as Gaffer), was also a diplomat, but he never managed to settle in one job, becoming a professor of Portuguese as well as of International Law and Political Science. Gaffer had a house in Spain and during the Civil War set up an ambulance unit to smuggle refugees out of the country. The ambulance consisted of an old motorbike to which he had strapped a wicker chair, and which he drove wearing white corduroy breeches and a white cloak. Despite these quirks, his work provided valuable humanitarian aid to people fleeing Francoist repression. There was a rebellious, restless, venturesome streak in Gerry's family – one of his uncles was a keen mountaineer, teaching the young George Mallory the basics of climbing, and himself reaching the top of Mont Blanc despite having a wooden leg. Gerry's father was a Communist sympathiser, a brilliant linguist and an inventor (some in the family claim he may have invented the precursor to the Bletchley Park deciphering machines). But he was an eccentric man, obsessed with alliteration, unreliable and prone to doing strange exercises involving violent leaping and dashing about with rugs furled around his waist. Below a puff of white hair his hawk-like face, arranged around a prominent nose, was scored with the same lips that on Gerry looked charming but that seemed on Gaffer to be a snarl. He was also unfaithful. Gerry's mother put up with her husband's infidelities and the fact that he had fathered an illegitimate son. She trailed in his wake, as he, with infuriating arrogance, instructed her to 'Pay, pack and follow.'

In choosing Elisabeth, Gerry was seeking a different path from the muddle and turbulence of his parents' marriage. For Elisabeth, Gerry held the promise of adventure, radicalism and of provoking her parents' disapproval of his less-than-conventional family. Perhaps they were each looking for their shadow: one wanting to be grounded by his love, and the other to be swept away by hers. For all their differences, they came from the same social class and had both lived nomadic lives within the same circles; and their marriage was firmly anchored by the taproots of love.

*

Elisabeth and Gerry's wedding

On the day of her wedding, 14 February 1939, Elisabeth awakes feeling calm. It is chilly but the weather has held. A maid knocks on her door and brings in breakfast, which Elisabeth is surprised she manages to devour. Aren't brides supposed to be so jangly they can't eat? She feels only a sense of excitement and the deep pleasure that comes with knowing you have made a good decision. She has a bath whilst everyone else flaps around her.

As she slithers into the long, fitted ivory silk dress Elisabeth's face breaks into a delighted smile. The service goes well and the couple emerge from the church for the official photographs. Gerry is emanating happiness, and Elisabeth smiles over her bouquet of lilies, voluptuously drooping tulips and lily-of-the-valley.

There are reports in the newspapers, which Elisabeth keeps safely in a scrapbook. The headlines like 'Bullet Brings the Bliss: Girl to Wed Man Who Probed Wound With Doorkey', and 'The Bullet and Latchkey Romance' have contributed to the narrative passed down to me and my siblings; they are the lighter, more colourful filaments of these life stories.

Elisabeth was glad that they had a proper wedding, before her father's new posting to Turkey, and before war broke out. She was aware that their ceremony was a luxury at this time. One of her friends was telephoned by her fiancé to say he was allowed out of his tank for half an hour and to meet him at a church, where he was in such a rush to get the wedding done that he took the skin off her finger jamming on the ring, before dashing back to his duties.

They had a proper honeymoon too. In a pile of letters from

Gerry to Elisabeth, I find a bill from a hotel in Sicily where they enjoyed their first days as newlyweds, as Europe skittered, like a lamb on ice, inexorably into war. Nestled in this curl of a bay, eating pasta, drinking fresh coffee, watching the boats sway gently on the smooth water, their world was peaceful.

*

A photograph of Gerry and Elisabeth leaving the church, freshly wed, stood for years on my mother's windowsill, framed by shadows and star-spattered skies. As a child, I scoured the picture for clues as to who these people really were, for something that could connect them to me. I would hold it, stroke the cold, dusty glass and ask my mother about her parents, enchanted by them and unable to grasp the horror of her loss. By the time she was thirteen, both my mother's parents had died, and it is only now, as I get to know more about Elisabeth and Gerry, that I begin to understand how starkly her life would have been divided into a before and an after.

And then comes the phone call. My mother's voice has become strange – crackly and brittle. She had a cold some weeks ago, but the scratchiness in her throat remained, and the doctor has finally sent her for a chest X-ray. She tells me the results: she has suspected stage four non-small-cell adenocarcinoma. Lung cancer. I hold the phone in one hand and look at the floorboards as the ground seems to be sucked away from me. Time collapses, and I'm back to the day, sixteen years ago, when, aged forty-eight (just four years older than I am now), she was diagnosed with bowel and ovarian cancer.

That time is hazy for me: I remember her seeming to shrink, becoming brittle and birdlike, her hair thinning and white, the rest of the family struggling to cope but not knowing how to reach each other, blundering around without our central compass. I remember visiting her in hospital, finding her under a yellow waffle blanket at the end of the ward, holding her hand because no words would come. After months of operations and savage chemotherapy, she was given the 'all clear'; but it seems that cancer was merely lingering in the darkness, waiting for its moment to blossom. Now I am there again, waiting for more news and a way to make sense of what is happening. She is sent for more tests.

One afternoon soon after that phone call, my mobile beeps: a text. *News not 2 good.* A tumour is growing on her left lung, twining itself somewhere between her heart and vocal chords, and this time, we are told, she will not survive. The cancer is inoperable, incurable; the oncologist tells her she has months to live. We scrabble for information, anything on which to peg our horror and grief as she begins treatment. The chemotherapy makes her feel worse than the illness and she stops having it after being told it will only prolong her life by six months.

It seems especially savage and poignant that just as I am beginning to piece Elisabeth's life back together, my mother is told hers is coming to an end.

3

Holland Park

To be done in the flat:

Drawing-room : Line drawers ✓   Cushion ? ✓
     Re-sort Rings ✓   Ket-curtain ✓
     Cut carpet ✓

Hall :   Book-case curtain ✓   Re-arrange bookcase
     Line drawer ✓   go thro' chest ✓
     Arrange books ✓

Dressing-room: Key for cupboard   Jumble sale ✓
Bath-room : Paint wood — & spare bed

Kitchen :   Dresser curtain ✓   Store boxes ✓
     Cupboard lock ✓

Bed-room : ~~many~~ Clean walls.   Visit ?   Make curtain
     Curtain for shoe-cupboard ✓   Store coat, linen chest

GARDEN : ~~BOXES TO~~ FOR MoSA : ~~STOW SUITCASES~~ : ~~WINE CUP~~

Polish Furniture.   { Accounts
Mend.   { Laundry   M.
 Accounts.   { Turning out
Flowers.   { Sewing   T.
Oddments
Floor   ∨   { Floor
go thro' things   { Furniture   W.
Sew
{ Extra cleaning   Extras
{ Painting
{ Floor etc.   —   Monday: Tidying, flowers.
Cooking   ~~Mend~~   Extras.
∨   Tuesday: Shopping.

                         Wednesday: Accounts.
your furs ✓   Paint   ~~Garden~~
diary   Floor ✓   Al Thursday: Mending.
Photographs   g's clothes ✓
          List everything   Friday: Gardening.
Put away winter clothes ..
garden .

ELISABETH AND GERRY'S FIRST MONTHS TOGETHER AS a married couple are spent in a rented flat in Holland Park, London. The next few lists in Elisabeth's book are all concerned with making a home. The book, and Elisabeth, settle – for now.

Thanks to the Internet, I am able immediately to find a picture of Gerry and Elisabeth's first flat as it is today: stuccoed, grand, with an elaborate iron awning curling above the entrance, windows in the roof and leafy trees dappling the pavement outside. A fine place from which to launch a new life, surrounded by their wedding presents and a little trepidation. Elisabeth uses her book of lists to channel this nervous energy, and notes down all the tasks to be done in the flat to make it comfortable. Over these pages, the book shifts from being a record or a way of remembering to becoming a template for efficient housekeeping. There is a sense of purpose and focus to these lists. She ticks off the jobs she has completed and assigns particular chores to certain days (Monday: tidying, flowers; Tuesday: shopping; Wednesday: accounts). She creates a list of names, addresses and phone numbers for all the people she will call upon to help her run her household: 'Garage, Builders, Upholstery, Daily…' She is consciously transforming herself into the embodiment of an organised married woman, and the book of lists becomes a reference point from which she will run her household, and to which she will turn in times of anxiety and bustle and joy.

Elisabeth's mother would have taught her the value of being organised, the necessity of keeping efficient and accurate records of possessions that might otherwise be lost. And there would also be an unspoken message: that sometimes you will be bored, unfulfilled, tired of being on view, desperately sad; and making a list might just save you. The wisdom of generations of women has long been passed down like this, whether showing someone how to keep accounts, or taking a daughter's hand and teaching her the ancient push and fold of kneading dough.

The flat that is now the focal point of Elisabeth's inventories is neat and tastefully simple in its decoration. The long hallway is divided in two, one end housing the dining table, with its silver jam pot and coffee jug, and the other is an entrance way, with a desk drenched in morning sunlight from the window behind. Elisabeth keeps flowers in a vase on the table in the sitting room, and sits at her bureau to write. Whenever I think of Elisabeth in this flat, she is writing – keeping up with her correspondence, or scribbling down notes to herself. She is a compulsive notebook-keeper, part of what Joan Didion describes as 'a different breed altogether, lonely and resistant rearrangers of things, anxious malcontents, children afflicted apparently at birth with some

presentiment of loss'. I am reminded of something Oliver
Sacks wrote about his need to 'think on paper', using whatever
scraps he could find to jot down ideas, lists, memories. He saw
this categorising as a way to 'fix in words' the slipperiness of
life and thoughts, a way to be truly 'ALIVE – hence universals
of Activity, organizing, adapting, but equally of individuality,
identity, diversity'. During the day, Elisabeth follows the light,
moth-like, tracking through the flat to find the perfect space
in which to compose her diary entries and lists. And herself.
When Gerry gets home from his job in the press office, he sits
on the small wooden chair next to the fireplace, tapping his
pipe on the mantelpiece and regaling Elisabeth with stories
of warmongering and political wrangling.

Gerry is frantically busy, drafting speeches and trying
to bring the country back from the brink, but by now it is
clear that war is almost inevitable. There is a heatwave and
the usual swelling and blossoming of spring, yet all this is
overshadowed by the prospect of what is coming. Elisabeth
captures this sense of foreboding: 'But how can one really
enjoy it? Supposing we are killed in a month or two? What is
the use of arranging a future?' Against the looming violence,
Elisabeth roots herself in her marriage: 'Just to be happy &
make Gerry happy. It's enough to do that – it's perfect, & I
never knew how much I should love it…I love waking up
in the morning & seeing the back of his head with two ears
sticking out, just nearby on the pillow.'

But she also needs a purpose outside the domestic realm.
In the summer of 1939 she takes a job at a social welfare
centre, and volunteers in a thrift shop. One weekend she and

Gerry go to stay at Cliveden, a large house perched above the Thames in Berkshire, home to Nancy Astor, and just across the river from Gerry's parents' house near Maidenhead. Elisabeth is struck by the grandness of the mansion and the eccentricity of the hostess: '...vases containing at least 60 lilies each, logs the size of trees burning in a huge fireplace, and Lady Astor herself shooting into the hall with a crack on her lips for each guest in turn – some of the cracks quite rude ones, too. The guests couldn't help hanging on Lady Astor's words, partly because she talked so loudly, and partly because she was extraordinarily funny. She whisked the ladies off after tea and shut them up in the library, ordered the men to go and thrash out the political situation, and with a parting word of mockery tornado-ed off to her sitting room. After dinner she suddenly whisked in a set of false teeth and started giving a lively imitation of the type of woman sent to entertain the troops. As she went skipping around and waving her legs in a very agile way, her velvet "tea-gown" suddenly fell open to the waist, exposing luxurious scanties and silk-stockings, much to everybody's amusement.' The next morning, Lady Astor sat painting her nails whilst her guests ate Sunday sausages.

After this brief sojourn with the Cliveden set and their dubious right-wing politics, Elisabeth and Gerry return to London and their work. Elisabeth finds herself dealing with a variety of complicated cases. On a single day, she helps the grandmother of a neglected young refugee, an aristocratic woman who was in trouble for throwing an egg at her grocer, and a woman with a three-year-old child suffering from a mental disorder. A life of contrasts, of dipping in and out of different worlds, glittering and carefree one minute, serious and responsible the next. For the first time in Elisabeth's life, home is now the one constant, and she pours her energy into giving it solidity.

Her 'Still Wanted for the Flat' list paints a vivid picture of Elisabeth and Gerry's home. The bath-salt bowl, coal scuttle, table brush and other things she has crossed off, as well as the backgammon board, potpourri, silver sauce boats and camping things to come...all these everyday objects would have their own stories to tell. As A. C. Grayling writes, 'Trifles are the texture of history; in minutiae lie truths, and more significance attaches to the myriad of events unobvious or apparently mundane than to single grand upheavals.' Coming after the pages and pages of items given to them as wedding gifts, this list of yet more objects is a stark reminder of how much *stuff* we surround ourselves with. It is as if Elisabeth is trying to anchor herself, to give this life she now has weight and permanence, even though she is aware that Gerry's next foreign posting could come at any moment.

In a previous list, Elisabeth instructs herself to 'List everything', and on the following pages of the book, she embarks on a comprehensive inventory, recording all their glass, linen and silver. I am struck by the mammoth task she has set herself and I wonder whether she was aware of the inherent futility of trying to corral all the disparate pieces of our lives into an orderly shape. Was she aware of a deeper reason for her constant lists? In one of her diary entries, I come across these lines: 'One of my faults is a feeling I must

Still wanted for flat:

Cushions ✓	Small Kodak
Rugs	Camping things
Long mirror ✓	Good torch
Small table ✓	Flap-jack
Rolling-board ✓	
Backgammon	
Cigarette-case ⎫ ✓	
Note-case ⎬ 8 ✓	
~~Coal scuttle~~ ✓	
~~Fire-irons~~ ✓	
· Eiderdown ✓ .	
~~Bread-board~~ ✓	
Pot-pourri ✓	
~~Table-brush~~	
Silver sauce-boats	
~~Bath-mat~~	
Cork bath mat ✓	
~~Pillows~~ ✓	
Hot-plate	
Stool	

always be <u>doing</u> something – not a bad feeling in some way, but hopeless when carried to such an extreme that one is always making out lists and organising oneself.' When I read this, I feel excited, as though Elisabeth has just answered my question. She did recognise her inability to be truly 'still' and she saw her list-making as part of this. But, unlike Elisabeth, I don't see this as a fault as much as a coping mechanism. It is a learned practice, carried on from generations before and passed down to my mother, with her lists of things she is knitting for her grandchildren and rambles she is planning; and to me, with my lists of books I feel I should have read, of important dates and places in Elisabeth's life, and the family Saturday chores that need to be ticked off.

The next list is just one of several spread over three pages that give a perfect snapshot of how scattered Elisabeth's life would become were it not for her book of lists. When faced with the complicated juggling act of making a home while being ready at any moment to uproot herself, lists like this one are essential props. As war has been declared and Gerry has not been told where they will be posted, Elisabeth begins making preparations for a move. In the first few months of 1940 there are earthquakes in Turkey (where Elisabeth's parents are now living), further German expansions into Europe, a war of propaganda, news of the Soviets machine-gunning civilians, a 'war of nerves'. For Elisabeth and Gerry, the future is impossible to predict: 'I should like to think that in another year we should be in some remote & sunny corner of the world. But who can tell <u>where</u> we shall be by then,' Elisabeth writes in her diary.

Furniture etc. stored at Pimms, North Street, Oxford

1 eiderdown (old)	10 x 12 ft. Turkey carpet
3 x 6 ft. oak bedstead	4.6 x 9 Persian ··
✗ 3 ft. mahogany chest of drawers	11.3 x 12.6 Turkey ··
16 stair rods & eyes	10.6 x 11.3 Persian ··
3 ft. mahogany Hall Table	3 Rugs from Spain. 3 Bath- Towels.
* 6 (?) prs. brown velour curtains	3 ·· " Mate.
✗ Small walnut bureau	2 Counterpanes?
3 ft. ·· Table	Furniture stored at Bishops.
? walnut musical box	2 Armchairs
4 ft. mahogany writing-table	Numerous pictures
6 pr. plated fish knives	✗1 Book-stand (to go on a table)
Case of fish servers	1 Big. Wardrobe cupboard, drawers
Large square settee	✗1 " C. of d. (needs painting)
Abt. 10 Medici prints	3 or 4 beds
? 4 Tier steamer	2 Dressing-tables
✗ Dinner-service (?)	4 Bedroom chairs
* lent to Holland St. & some at 71.	1 Book-case (damaged)
	1 Round table
	1 Small desk

Gerry's bureau | Several small tables
Side-board (card-table) ✗ stool
Mirror of dressing-table

She must keep track of where certain belongings are stored, so that when and if they return to London, they can reassemble the life they had just begun. Any move away will always be temporary, just as any return 'home' will be calibrated by a silently ticking clock marking the beats until the next upheaval.

From furniture like the oak bedstead to household linens and dusters, these are mundane yet precious items, things she wants to keep safe. They are things that constitute home. Some of them feel strangely intimate – the twenty-four face towels, Gerry's flannel pyjamas and fourteen pairs of woollen socks – while some appear to be surplus paraphernalia that she just can't quite get rid of, like the custard cups and egg dishes. Trunks, old Revelation leather suitcases and cardboard boxes are filled with these objects and sent to various places to await Elisabeth's return.

These lists of Elisabeth's are useful in revealing the complexities of our relationships with 'things'. Lists enclose objects, they give them a different, less transient space within which to exist, and reveal the emotional connections we have with them. Susan Sontag described her own compulsion to make lists as a way to confer value and guarantee existence for the things she notes down: 'I *perceive* value, I *confer* value, I *create* value, I even create – or guarantee – *existence*. Hence my compulsion to make "lists". The things…won't exist unless I signify my interest in them by at least noting down their names. Nothing exists unless I maintain it…This is an ultimate, almost subliminal anxiety.' Elisabeth was constantly selecting and culling objects with each house move, deciding not only which to take with her but also which to include in her lists. In contrast to today's mass-produced, disposable consumer goods, Elisabeth's family shipped the same refrigerator with them around the world. Objects and furniture are passed on through families, treasured links with the past. There are stories within these things, be they inkstands or wall brackets, and within the lists that provide them a liminal place to live forever.

In my research at the Mass Observation Archive (a collection that was founded in 1937 containing material about everyday life), I find some delightful lists of the objects Elisabeth's contemporaries had on their mantelpieces, a glimpse into her time. Some observers wrote in great detail, giving measurements and diagrams, and others noted rather extraordinary objects like a crumpled cigarette card used as a toothpick, a pair of dissecting forceps, a wooden ashtray guarded by a grotesque orange pelican, a whale's ear bone and a small piece of chair. Stripped of their context, these things have an intensity – the possibility of a story, of reading something into the object.

The artist Joseph Cornell captured this sense of possibility, of the evocation of memories associated with objects, in his shadow boxes. The glass-fronted boxes filled with ephemera, collage and found objects become a portal through which the past can be accessed. He was also a prolific keeper of notes, images, inventories of sources of inspiration and accounts of everyday life – what he termed the 'métaphysique d'ephemera'.

There can be something stark and revealing about the objects in a simple list. Take, for example, the list of belongings confiscated by the Soviet secret police, the NKVD, on the arrest of the Russian writer Isaac Babel in 1939. Suspected of being a spy for the French, Babel eventually confessed to espionage after being mistreated and tortured. His possessions were gathered up and noted down: a life collected. Amongst the objects you might expect to find in the home of a writer (manuscripts, books, letters), there was also a 'duck for the bath'. A poignant reminder that this was a person – a man who perhaps kept a rubber duck as a keepsake from his childhood, or had a playful nature.

In writing a list we capture a moment in which the objects we are itemising play a specific role in our life (or someone else's). But our possessions also affect our sense of well-being, and the way we manage them can profoundly affect our levels of happiness. We rearrange our homes, moving furniture around in much the same way we place objects on a list. The physical act and aesthetic ritual of making a list helps us to manage our feelings (of loss, dislocation, of being overwhelmed) as well as to record our past; they are a form of autobiography through objects and emotions.

*

Gerry wrote Elisabeth a touching letter from the flat before they were married: 'Darling I feel I must write you a letter from our new house. I do think it's nice, and I hope to God you'll be happy here. I'll do my very best to see you are, but I'm such an awful fool that I'm rather frightened.' I find this letter surprisingly moving. I think it is because he tried so hard, but she was *not* always happy, in fact she was sometimes deeply unhappy. This is what makes these lists so bittersweet. Reading of their hopeful, trembling new life together, I feel a stabbing frustration – I can't help but constantly fast-forward to the end. Although I am no longer sure where that end is. Is it the end of Elisabeth's life? Or is it beyond that? Does it end with my mother? Or me? Or my children, skipping and tripping down their own paths?

Gerry and Elisabeth's marriage was not without its challenges or difficulties, but their relationship flourished in a world on a precipice, like a tiny but deep-rooted edelweiss clinging to the rocks. Gerry was Elisabeth's rescuer: from bullets, from depression, from dependence on her peripatetic parents…Ultimately, Gerry could not save Elisabeth, but I realise that part of me is trying to.

*

Four years after I try on the fragile gold dress, after I first open the pages of Elisabeth's book of lists, my mother is living life with the heightened awareness and energy that only the dying can really know. She has embarked on an informal programme of juicing, prayer, walks, retreats and open discussions about her death. She is living with this abhorrent lump, with the awkward voice and shortness of breath, yet we are all suspended in a surreal limbo, grateful for her being well and alive and all the incredible things she is, but knowing at some point she will be taken from us.

She begins to leave slowly, in increments of varying obviousness. First, there is the sorting out of her clothes, of papers and emails and clutter. Then she gives me two small pieces of yellow paper on which she has written two prayers. Despite not believing in God, I carry them with me every day, keeping her close. We have had a last family summer holiday together. Then another. And, unbelievably, another. All this time that I am grieving, I am discovering Elisabeth, trying to understand how it must have been for my mother to lose her so young. That loss was so deep and shattering that my own sorrow feels somehow fraudulent, but I feel it nonetheless. I am trying to heal my mother, and also to understand how she could leave me.

As my mother's illness progresses, so I plunge deeper into Elisabeth's world. I feel myself beginning to sink so far into the story that I don't want to come up for air. My mother represents one strand of the spidery thread with which I am spinning Elisabeth's story. She is my connection to everything, my reference point, my beginning. And she is unravelling. So I hold more tightly to the other end of the thread the yellowing paper and cracking cloth spine of Elisabeth's book of lists. It feels like the faster I spin, the further my mother slips from me, but the closer I get to Elisabeth.

In the book of lists, I search for patterns, ways that lead back from Elisabeth to make sense of my mother, and myself, and I clutch at things that we three share: our freckle-smattered arms, our mutual love of almond chocolate, a desire to write, and the urge to make lists. The time I spend in Elisabeth's strange world of inventories and beauty and wildness and sadness becomes increasingly precious, as though by reimagining Elisabeth's life, I might prolong my mother's too.

4

Madrid

July 16ᵗ   Madrid.

Mques.
　Casa   Valdes ✓   Ciswells ✓   Stuttart ✓
Snta. Aranda   ✓   Goodens ✓
　　Kobé   ✓   Crains   ✓
Condese de la Maya ✓   Baker
Angelita Villaverde NO   Hamiltons ✓
Primo di Rivera   Starkey   ✓
Duquesa de Sueca.   Reeverys ✓
Pilar   Pears   ✓
Merry de Vals   ✓   Tencken   ✓

　　1 Bottle Sherry   Sherry
Drink: 1 Bottles Gin   ⎧ Orange blossom
　1   "   Vermouth   ⎨ Martinis
　1   "   Whisky   ⎩ Whisky
　　3 Siphas Soda-water   Orangeade.
　　　　　　　　　　　　　　　　　ICE
　　Orange Juice & water.   Cheese straws
　1 Lemon for Martinis.   Stuffed eggs
　　　Cigarettes, matches.   Sardine balls
　　　Flowers.   Biscuits, plain & sweet
　　　　　　　　　　　　　　　　　　"   with cheese
　　　　　　　　　　　　　　　　Dates, olives, nuts
　　　　　　　　　　　　　　　　Sweets.

IN MAY 1940, GERRY AND ELISABETH FINALLY HEAR WHERE they're being posted: Madrid. The city had been a focal point of resistance during the Spanish Civil War of 1936–9, but with the surrender of Madrid in March 1939, Franco declared his triumph over the Republican forces and their allies, establishing a fascist regime that would last nearly forty years.

Gerry and Elisabeth have only a matter of days to make arrangements for the move to Spain, and she is busy organising the letting of their Holland Park flat (where they have lived for little more than a year), buying food and arranging for Gerry's uniform to be let out a couple of inches so he can do it up. She goes to Harrods and tries on several garments from the 'Younger Set' department for herself, buys Horlicks and Alka-Seltzer and arranges for their provisions to be sent by boat. She is in a 'whirl of lists & arrangements, and G is so tied up with the ambassador's plans that he cannot attend to personal affairs at all...During the ¼ of an hour when he was having his hair cut the telephone went 7 times.' Along with a few suitcases full of their belongings and Elisabeth's book of lists, the couple set off.

Their journey begins in a government Rolls Royce, as they are accompanying the new ambassador, Sir Samuel Hoare, and his wife, Maud. Hoare has ordered that they fly by private aeroplane, despite the massive cost, and the diplomatic party are loaded into a huge aircraft, while the typist and detective are packed off by boat (to keep within weight restrictions). It is a frightening journey: they have to fly low, Elisabeth constantly expects they will be shot down, and she and Gerry are pea-green with airsickness. Once they arrive in Lisbon, there is a problem collecting their luggage, including Gerry's sword (part of his diplomat's uniform), which was travelling loose, and the ambassador's sword, which was in a golf bag. The ship transporting their other belongings (including a three-month supply of toothpaste), plus the typist and detective, also faced a perilous voyage. The ship ahead of it had been torpedoed, and their own watchman sighted the periscope of a submarine in the salty depths.

Portugal remains neutral throughout the war, so Lisbon is one of the only European cities that continues to function normally. After a few days there, the party is ready to fly on to Madrid, store-lists and possessions duly sorted out. One of those who waves them off at the aerodrome is General Franco's brother. When they arrive in Madrid, they are faced with boiling sun, the aftermath of pro-Axis demonstrations and demands for the British to return Gibraltar to Spain. Elisabeth is not impressed with the embassy: 'The bath-room arrangements are dreadful, & it is v small…It was packed with refugees during the war, who worked havoc with the furniture, & left the whole place infested with bugs. The

Ambassador's study was destroyed by a bomb that went right through it…'

Like a boxer retiring to his corner, bruised and disfigured, patting down his body to find where it is broken, Spain is reeling from the years of civil war. It is a predominantly rural economy, where most of the countryside is farmed using ancient, basic agricultural practices. This landscape, dotted with olive groves and vineyards, was the scene of vicious fighting during the conflict. The early years of Franco's rule are characterised by political purges, repression, economic problems resulting from the loss of workers and destruction of infrastructure during the war, mass executions and 'disappearances' of opposition supporters. The country also sees a decline in industrial and agricultural production, which combines with a severe drought to produce near-famine levels of starvation.

The city in which Elisabeth makes her new home witnessed some of the fiercest and bloodiest fighting during the Civil War. It is a city in aftershock, patrolled by the *civiles* (the fascist police), pervaded by an atmosphere of deep suspicion and fear. She picks her way through the city's bones: buildings are twisted skeletons, shops boarded up, the roads are pocked with bomb craters, women in black move like ghosts through the gashed streets, most of the trees have been axed for fire wood and shanty villages have sprung up around the city.

My grandparents arrive into what Hoare described as a politically 'explosive atmosphere'. Britain is at war with Germany, and as its official representatives Gerry and the other diplomats have to tread a careful line. The Franco government is riven with internal disputes and disagreements about whether Spain should join the international conflict, and which side they should support. Officially, the country is a non-belligerent, but it does provide some support to the Axis countries, who assisted Franco in his bid for power. Gerry's task, and the principal strategy at the British embassy under the new ambassador, is to keep Spain out of the war and retain control of Gibraltar and the surrounding seas. The Madrid embassy is full of spies gathering intelligence about Franco's relationship with the Nazis, and government figures are bribed to further the British cause in keeping Spain out of the war.

The embassy is also an important gathering-point for strategic information, and is a funnel for refugees escaping persecution in Nazi-occupied countries. With the covert agreement of the Franco government, the British are able to get refugees across the borders into Spain and evacuate them out of Europe, mainly through Portugal. Madrid is home to wealthy aristocratic foreigners and Spaniards, many of whom had worked for the resistance during the Civil War and want to continue to obstruct the Franco regime. There is a different atmosphere here to what Elisabeth experienced in China: the locals and expats are more able to work together, and there is less of a sense of 'them and us'.

I find a lovely story about the embassy tea room, run in Elisabeth's time by Margarita Taylor. It became a sheltering point for these refugees waiting to be smuggled off the coast as part of an elaborate but largely improvised escape route. The plan worked like this: a doctor in a Spanish prisoner-of-war camp near the border with France declared, falsely, that thousands of the prisoners were in poor health or that there was an outbreak of some invented epidemic and therefore the prisoners should be released. They then made their way to Madrid, often to Margarita Taylor's tea room, where they met people from the British embassy who helped them escape from Europe.

During Gerry's time in Madrid the people involved in the smuggling of refugees are putting themselves at considerable risk and the operation will not be talked about even after the war ends. Knowing what I do now about the covert operations at the embassy and Gerry's father's assistance in getting refugees safely out of Spain, I think it very possible that Gerry was also involved in helping the resistance against the Franco government. The situation for all involved is not only personally but also internationally perilous – if the Germans discover that Spain is not really acting neutrally, the flickering distrust between the two powers will escalate into all-out war.

While Gerry is keen to make his mark at the embassy, Elisabeth is beginning her new role as a diplomat's wife. With her upbringing as a diplomat's daughter who has moved constantly throughout her life, Elisabeth knows that she must fully inhabit this new place. She must set out her belongings on a sideboard in someone else's house, she must speak a new language when buying vegetables at the market, she must befriend new people and dazzle others, she must not look back at what she is leaving behind. Her book of lists is a way to manifest this forward-looking energy, to harness the power of planning as a means of shoring herself up against the difficulties of making another new start. Its pages record the components of her life shuffled and shipped, her hopes and expectations grounded in the ink – and she will not be without it for the next thirteen years.

*

Life at the embassy in Madrid is dominated by the unpopular ambassador and his wife. Samuel Hoare was a relative of Elisabeth's (he was married to her aunt), a difficult, boorish man who had worked previously in the Intelligence Services. Later, when asked about her time here, Elisabeth tells a friend, 'It was made almost unbearable by the Hoares', to which her friend exclaims, 'Really, the whores? Were they a terrible problem?' Gerry is bored, his days taken up mostly with running errands for Hoare or cyphering. Conversations in the offices are punctuated by code words like 'TOCK ACK BABY', and the staff live in a strange vacuum under a regime that they deplore. There is a febrile energy about the place, and constant rumours that Spain is about to declare war on Britain. The staff know they may be sent home at any time. When France falls to the Nazis in June 1940, all parties are cancelled and staff are ordered to stop unpacking food. It is hard to plan more than a few hours ahead.

After a tricky time settling in and suffering with stomach problems and bed bugs, Elisabeth's daily life is just as busy and unpredictable as Gerry's. She works hard, organising social gatherings and dealing with a variety of minor crises, like trying to track down stolen petrol coupons, having to rush out and buy bathing suits for the ambassador and his wife, establishing why the wrong kind of flour has been sent, and fixing the refrigerator. She takes driving lessons and learns Spanish, she entertains visitors, then scathingly records what she really thought of some of them in her diary: 'A terrible example of the aristocracy gone to seed came to lunch: Millicent, Duchess of Sutherland, en route from France to America with her Pekinese. She was rather mountainous, & curiously dressed at the extremities: a white felt tennis hat on her head, no stockings, but white socks & sandals. Round her neck was strung a metal plaque with "Sans peur" boldly engraved on it.'

In the context of the situation facing most Spaniards – chronic food shortages, repression, fear and hopelessness for the future – embassy staff have a fairly easy time. Elisabeth worries that there won't be enough food to entertain guests and that their stash of cigarettes will run out: 'Certainly it is a nightmare in Madrid now, as one can't buy meat, eggs, oil or lentils, let alone flour etc.' She is also concerned about the plight of the Spanish people. In her diary, she records that merchants have been hoarding food, hoping to sell their produce abroad for huge profits, but when the food went bad, they threw around 100,000 kilos of it into the sea in front of a starving crowd. As long as the supplies from the Army & Navy store in England can get through, the staff will not starve, and Elisabeth also learns to look elsewhere. She recounts an expedition with a friend into the countryside to buy food on the black market – it is illegal to move food between the provinces, but people in rural areas secretly sell surplus food in order to get by and avoid giving it to the government (one woman poured away pints of surplus milk each day rather than hand it over to Food Control officers).

It is risky, this trade, and people are understandably nervous of selling to strangers in case they are spies, but Elisabeth's friend manages to swap some cakes and chocolate for twelve eggs, and buys three hams from the administrator at the Duke of Alba's house. The friend also arranges a secret assignation to obtain more eggs in a remote hamlet, and visits some obscure elderly relatives of hers who have lentils for sale. Following a complicated map, they find a tiny telephone exchange, which is full of villagers offering lentils, beans and chickpeas, with hens and pigs wandering about, and where nobody answers the permanently ringing telephone; they manage to barter for fifteen dozen eggs, which they hide in some straw inside a suitcase.

Gerry and Elisabeth have to send their shoes to Lisbon to be repaired due to the lack of leather available in Spain, and there are also petrol shortages across the country. Despite the embassy allowance, running out of petrol is always a possibility on any journey. On one occasion Gerry has to syphon petrol from a colleague's car into a pudding bowl, but so much is swallowed or spilt the car has to be shunted the last mile home with Elisabeth at the wheel: '…so I arrived triumphantly at the petrol pump, resting snugly on Malcolm's bumper (which somehow sounds vaguely indecent) & Gerry instructing me how to steer properly'.

Elisabeth seems to relish the challenges of making do in these unusual and adventure-filled circumstances, and there is a lightness to her mood that was not apparent in London. When the Duke and Duchess of Windsor pass through Madrid, Gerry and Elisabeth have to book them rooms at the Ritz, but the manager is underwhelmed at the prospect: 'The Manager was frightfully rude about them, & held up his hands in horror, saying they'd already got Madeleine Carroll, & that was quite enough in the way of celebrities.' Elisabeth is also unimpressed: 'The Windsors dined "quietly". She was beautifully dressed, but seemed v. insincere & artificial. He twitched more than ever, & began his sentences with "When I was King…"…The Windsors are an awful bore, as they give G. a lot of extra work, & they <u>won't</u> go back to England, in spite of a flood of wills summoning them back at once.'

Elisabeth was masterful at capturing people's foibles and peculiarities. She saw the ridiculous in situations and had an eye for detail which makes me think she was intending to use her diaries as source material for a writing project. Why else note events such as this: 'My day was made by Mrs Weddell, whose knickers fell off at a tea-party the Ambassadress was giving on the verandah. They were curious ones, too, with no sides. "I don't like to be bunchy over the hips, so I have them this way," she said, holding them up for all to see, before she stuffed them away in her bag. Incredible old body!' Elisabeth's sense of fun and lightheartedness shine through these anecdotes and descriptions, and I sometimes feel as if she were sitting across the table from me, in her old age, recounting tales from her travels: 'I enjoyed the trip to La Granja & back. One could do that drive countless times without its being dull – it is lovely nearly all the way. But there is no denying that 1½ hrs. each way is a long way to go for a glass of unpalatable hock-cup & a stale éclair.'

*

For all her sense of mischief, Elisabeth is proving to be a consummate hostess. The list at the start of this chapter is one of many party lists in Elisabeth's book. She has recorded the guests invited, and the food and drink to be served. It seems a fairly modest party – although she has altered the quantity of gin from one to two bottles, in anticipation of the amount that is usually drunk at these occasions. It is easy to see why someone like Gerry develops unhealthy drinking habits, his job requiring so much socialising and entertaining. The food is not elaborate, reflecting the problems of catering for extra people when supplies are scarce. Sometimes these embassy parties might be the guests' only chance of getting properly fed: Elisabeth writes of the difficulties some guests had in feeding their families, how the children 'usually breakfast off a piece of dry bread – no eggs, coffee or butter. And when they come back from school at the end of the morning they are so exhausted that they lap down Vermouth as a stimulant, knowing that there will be v. little for lunch.' The guests attending the party in this list don't look as though they would have such problems, however. There is a countess and a duchess, relics of an age when some of Spain's titled gentry could travel half way across the country without leaving their own properties, and when one duke used to have lunch and dinner for twenty prepared in all his country houses in case he felt like turning up. Those profligate times have passed, yet to many local people the foreigners in Madrid appear to be living in similar luxury.

One man on the list, Walter Starkey (usually spelt Starkie – I'm not sure why Elisabeth uses this spelling), is an eccentric figure at the embassy. He is a cultural representative involved in setting up the British Institute in Madrid – a place where the Spanish can enjoy a shared love of music and culture, and therefore retain their cultural ties to Britain – part of the diplomatic effort to keep Spain from joining the war. Elisabeth writes that Starkie once rode ten miles on a donkey with a fiddle on one thigh and a staff named 'Joyeuse' propped against the other. Many of the embassy employees seem similarly quirky: one was once so drunk that he remained asleep whilst being shaved by a barber, and another got into a dispute with a smuggler: 'The argument was punctuated by refreshing draughts of gin, & by the gun-runner firing patterns on the wall of the room with his revolver. Lively times, these.'

In addition to organising and hosting parties, Elisabeth often plunges into the depths of the city to read to a blind man called Mr Hick; she takes Spanish dancing lessons, enjoys shopping and exploring the junk shops, with music from cracked gramophones playing in the background, and going to the Prado to look at Goya's paintings. She visits El Rastro, a street market where desperate people sell trinkets and jewellery (much of which was stolen during the Civil War), and rummages alongside wealthy Madrileños hunting amongst the junk to find their family heirlooms and treasures. In the tattered boxes, she sees the tarnished glint of a lost world. On one occasion, fed up with the petty duties she has been made to undertake at the embassy, she 'pounced off to Balenciaga & bought 3 models. They fitted me exactly, & I loved them, & they weren't really expensive.' I detect a twinge of guilt here, spending money on clothes when there is so much hardship around, but Elisabeth always took great pride in her appearance, and, as a diplomat's wife, was expected to be well turned out. I wonder what happened to all these beautiful clothes. Where did they end up – who is wearing them now?

The embassy staff attend concerts and go to the cinema, and are also treated to occasional entertainment. A notable visitor is 'Gerry's Australian whip-cracking protégé', who is passing through on his way to Tangier. The man, a Lieutenant Colonel Holman James, aka Fred Lindsay, is a well-known performer, thrilling audiences with his skills with a stock whip. Elisabeth witnessed his impromptu performance to about forty people gathered in the embassy garden:

'Making a noise like a number of machine-guns he slashed about with his 30 foot leash, & then did remarkable tricks – tearing sheets of paper in half, whilst 2 of the typists held them in position: he tore the German newspaper by degrees till there remained only a piece the size of ½ a postage stamp. This he stuck on the end of my nose, & proceeded calmly to flick it off with one stroke of his whip, standing yards and yards away from me. He cracked the whip so that it coiled round a typist's neck, & so on. All extremely staggering – & we needed a lot of drink afterwards.'

Like much of what happens at the embassy, this performance has a political agenda: the man is travelling on behalf of the Ministry of Information to impress the Moroccans with the marvels of the Commonwealth nations, their strength and prowess supposedly embodied in the cracks of his whip.

For all the emphasis on soft diplomacy and displays of cultural bravado, it is impossible to ignore the brutal reality of Franco's Spain. Elisabeth is aware of the assassinations and Gestapo-style methods used by the government to control and exact revenge on its opponents. She describes the arrest of Miss Ritchie, a British typist, who was taken from her hotel and made to spend the night on a hard chair in a prison cell, with numerous rats and no food. She notes, 'This type of thing is happening all over Spain: and we sit down under it in the most sickening way.' A flash here of Elisabeth's gutsiness and disinclination to do what she is told. She is equally unflappable during her own confrontations with Franco's police: 'Coming home from dinner last night some figures stepped across the road, quite near our house, & tried to stop the car: we drove firmly on. But whilst unlocking the front gate there was a thud of feet behind us & five "Himmler" police all with bayonets closed in around us. They asked to see our identity cards. And when we asked why the only answer they could give was "Porche, porche". We thought it a bit hard, not being allowed into one's own house without being charged by the police.'

Elisabeth later describes how she, Gerry and a friend called Bob are followed out of the city by two policemen when they go on a picnic. The men make no attempt to conceal themselves, and Elisabeth's party hatch a plan to shake off their pursuers: 'Then up the pass (still sleuthed) till we came to a nice spot for a walk, at the top of the El Paular valley. We plunged off up hill (the sleuths being Spanish & idle preferred to remain waiting in their car)…When we got back to the car we saw all the sleuths were fast asleep in their Fiat. So v. quietly we drifted away, leaving them still asleep. We'd got some way down the pass, round half a dozen or so hair-pin bends, when we thought we heard a hoot behind us. It now seemed fright-fully exciting, & we were determined to evade the sleuths. So we tore on to the bottom of the pass, & took a cart-track into the woods & hid ourselves & Ford neatly behind some bracken. After waiting patiently for 5 minutes we decided, as nothing had happened, that we must have imagined the hoot, & that they were probably still snoring away in happy unconscious-ness at the top of the pass. So we backed laboriously out of the bracken & towards the road: at precisely the same moment as we reached it the sleuths appeared round the bend above us, pelting along for all they were worth. It was too infuriating: another 60 seconds & they would have gone pelting past our hiding place. However, we got the better of them on the next pass, as they broke down & we sailed on, leaving them stuck quite 20 miles from the nearest garage!'

I love reading this. I love her glee and the way the word 'sleuth' slips mockingly from the lips. I love her playfulness and humour; I find myself willing her down that mountain. Despite the dangers of this place, Elisabeth shows resilience, perhaps stemming in part from her sense of duty: they have a job to do and are not going to be intimidated out of doing it.

But the longer they stay in Madrid, the more unpleasant the atmosphere becomes and the more difficult it is to keep their spirits strong. They live in close proximity to German people, some civilians and some military personnel, and have to endure taunts and gloating about the progress of the war. Gerry is also singled out personally, thanks to his father's vocal support of some Communist ideals, and is himself accused of being a highly 'dangerous militant Communist'. At a bullfight, surrounded by dust and blood, he is attacked by the baying crowd and nearly arrested for not joining in the Nazi salute. Another time, when a German spy is discovered in the British embassy, Gerry is taken to the police station for questioning, perhaps because of his previous posting in Berlin and his less-than-diffident attitude towards his superiors. He is frustrated by the mindlessness of his daily work, feeling he is being underused and disagreeing with what he sees as the British policy of 'pandering' to Franco. Gerry and Elisabeth are also tired of living in the embassy itself, where there is a disagreeably gossipy atmosphere and they are unable to separate work and home. Elisabeth describes how one evening they are sitting eating ravioli and cabbage, she wearing her dressing gown, when the Greek minister and his wife turn up, two weeks late for a cocktail party. They begin to long for a new posting.

*

To escape the heat and difficulties of life in Madrid, Elisabeth and Gerry make frequent trips into the countryside. She uses her list book to note the items they will need, the book slipping easily from being used for professional purposes to the personal.

Things for Camping.

Tent, ground-sheet, beds.
Blankets + Pillows.
Flit, midge-stuff, iodine, toilet-paper, torch.
Washing things, including Towels & soap & basin.
Matches + Paper.
Kettle, frying-pan, saucepan, large spoon.
Coats + sweaters + mackintoshes.
Books, Dice, X-words, cigarettes.
Picnic basket, tin-opener, cork-screw + string.
Food: Wine + water: butter, tea, bread, sausages,
sardines, eggs, jam, milk, salt pepper + mustard
Eggs Fruit & salad. Olives. Cheese + biscuits. Sweets.
Tinned stuff. Macaroni. Tomatoes.

Hotel Holiday.

Cheque-book + money for tips. Our-es-thing, Cigarettes + matches.
Books. Letter things. Dice. Chess-board. Ping-pong. Corkscrew
Pillow. Soap & bath essence. Butter, chocolate, hedging things,
towels, washing, pyjamas! Knitting & sewing ... Clock.
Sleeping tablets etc ... Abba ... Hot water bottle ... Cards.
Rug.

Some of Elisabeth's lists reflect a world that seems far from my own – the endless list of opulent wedding presents, the cocktail parties for foreign dignitaries – but her travel lists for camping and hotel holidays seem classless and time-less. I love Elisabeth's exoticism and glamour, but I also love that she knits and wears pyjamas and packs 'midge stuff'. Her story is at once unusual and universal.

The things Elisabeth packs for camping are simple, pared-down, and neatly ordered into rows according to category: items for entertainment are chiefly crosswords, dice and cigarettes; cooking equipment is a frying pan, saucepan and a spoon. The food she takes is also basic, though it must feel hard-won and precious, given the severe food shortages.

On one particular venture into the Spanish sierra, their journey to the campsite starts badly. She and Gerry had planned to use mules to explore the mountains north-west of Madrid, but when the muleteer arrives, the mules are tacked up for riding rather than carrying luggage. After a sweaty struggle, the muleteer finally manages to balance their two suitcases, tent, camp beds, food and bottles of wine precari-ously on the backs of the animals.

After moving just two yards, one mule's load falls off completely, and the other takes advantage of the pause in proceedings to drop its head to eat the grass, which causes all its luggage to slip off as well. The mules are reloaded and the now decidedly tetchy procession walks on. Five minutes later, the luggage falls off again, and after one hour they have only managed to move a quarter of a mile. The first mule then rears, scattering the contents of the food box (those sardines

The overburdened mule

and olives, the jam and eggs) into the pine trees, and the girth on the second mule snaps, pitching his load once more to the ground. Hot, frustrated and furious, Gerry and Elisabeth eventually abandon the mules and go back to get their car. She writes of driving out from Madrid, past families threshing corn and donkeys pulling boxes driven by small boys, of screaming cicadas and of walking amongst the tangled debris left after the Civil War.

I have a photograph of this camping trip. Looking closely, I recognise the objects in the picture from the 'Things for Camping' list and I am as delighted as if I were seeing a picture of an old friend rather than a frying pan.

*

It is morning. Elisabeth crouches on a patch of dusty soil, draping some clothes on a rock to dry. A canvas tent flaps

Camping in the Sierra de Guadarrama

behind her, and nearby a kettle splutters over a fire. She fetches the butter from its makeshift cellar in a shallow rock pool beneath a boulder, and slices a pat into a frying pan. Dressed in a simple frock, short socks and pumps, she is relieved to escape the suffocating heat of Madrid and the stresses of embassy life. The tent is pitched on a small green island in the middle of a trout stream, surrounded by pine forest that radiates out into a valley, and then mountains. It is a secluded place, held in the wide stony arms of the Sierra de Guadarrama. Trenches and gun placements thread across the peaks of the mountains like man-made scars. Gerry has been sleeping in a hammock that has sagged to the ground and completely enveloped him, like a holey cocoon. He is at home by the water, the sounds of the river echoing the Thames running next to his boyhood home.

Elisabeth begins making breakfast, frying sausages in the butter and brewing coffee, ready for when he awakes. She breathes in the dry air, thick with the scent of lavender and thyme. There is a different silence here: a stillness and quiet totally unlike the shocked hush that has descended over Madrid.

While breakfast is cooking, they wash in the icy river, their skin smarting with the cold. Elisabeth gets out of the water with a shiver, leans back on a rock and closes her eyes. The dappled light casts shadows across her eyelids and she feels a sense of contentment. Gerry joins her, pulling on his trousers, the fabric sticking slightly to his damp legs, and lights a cigarette. From his pocket, he unfurls a piece of paper and begins to compose a limerick.

Later, they cook ham in red wine over the fire and a farmer passes by as he brings his cows up from milking to graze the rich mountain pastures, watching the foreigners with suspicious eyes that have seen too much. As the mellow clopping of the cowbells recedes Elisabeth wonders about this place, this country that has cleaved in two, where people still disappear and where atrocities that would have seemed unimaginable a few years before have become part of life. The landscape, too, is damaged – buildings demolished by shelling, trenches gouged out of the earth – and desiccated after a drought. Elisabeth and Gerry's little island is a tiny oasis. Out of this bloodied and battered land there rises a desperation that sparks in Elisabeth a strong desire to create *life*. Perhaps she will try for a baby.

*

Elisabeth and Gerry have little time together, as he is so busy with his work, and trips like these provide a welcome chance to be alone and to relax. For Elisabeth, part of the pleasure of these holidays must have been in the planning, in anticipating all the items she and Gerry might need to put work and the war and Madrid behind them. Not many other lists in her book contain ellipses, and I can almost see Elisabeth's mind racing from scene to scene, imagining the different moments the holiday might hold and trying to jot things down as she thought of them: 'Riding things, tweeds, woollens, pyjamas!…knitting and sewing…clock. Sleeping tablets, etc…' I am amused to see that her 'own sherry' was clearly an essential. (Joan Didion also listed bourbon as an essential on her own minimal packing list.) The list invokes evenings sitting around a fire in a whitewashed, creeper-covered hotel, listening to the wireless before it gets turned off by an overzealous maître d' (foreign news is forbidden), or an image of Elisabeth sipping sherry wearing the *abba* she had had made in Persia, the scent of jasmine hanging in the air.

There are other adventures, sometimes without Gerry. Elisabeth joins a performing troupe who are to be sent to Gibraltar to entertain the British troops there. The embassy holds auditions, which seem to involve lots of typists getting drunk on the free booze and various odd Spaniards wandering in unaware of what an audition is, but hoping for some food. Once the group has been selected, there follows a great deal of organisation, sorting out visas, etc., and finally the troupe flies to Gibraltar. I am surprised that Elisabeth was chosen, after reading a note from her sister Alethea in which she snortingly declares that Elisabeth couldn't sing a note, but Elisabeth had always been a keen actor and was involved in many informal performances at embassies as she was growing up. Perhaps she was just better than the non-English-speaking elderly woman who turned up to audition. The show starts shakily: the curtain is lowered too early during the 'Strip Tease' song and has to be raised again for Elisabeth's last two songs. Things seem to go better for the next few performances, and her time in Gibraltar is spent drinking whisky, dancing and talking until way past curfew with various RAF men. Most of the local women have been evacuated, so Elisabeth and her colleagues attract a lot of attention. They are shown around *HMS Renown* and are overcome with excitement on seeing the bakery, with the 1,000 loaves of white bread it produces daily – a contrast to the food situation in Madrid.

Reminders of the war are never far away. Elisabeth writes of the extensive bomb damage Gibraltar has suffered, and one night she is caught in an air raid. She and a friend shelter in a hotel basement 'packed with officers, & also a lot of panic-stricken Gibraltarians who sat around with their heads in their hands looking as if their last hour had come. The noise from the guns outside was terrific…We heard the plop of a bomb every now & then too. But after a gin-fizz apiece we felt distinctly braver.'

Having left England before bombs began falling from the skies, this is Elisabeth's first experience of such an attack, and she seems to hold her nerve. She discovers later that a bomb missed the *Renown* by only twenty yards. An unexploded bomb lands a few yards behind the house in which she is staying. Her room is pronounced unsafe, as it is full of shrapnel and plaster and the bomb could go off at any moment. She sleeps in the dining room, with the other guests bedding down in the hall, and they are all provided with tin hats. Two days after she leaves Gibraltar, she hears that a couple she had dinner with there have been killed.

Back in Spain, in October 1940 Elisabeth goes on a trip to see the Alcázar fortress in Toledo, a huge palace that was besieged by the Republicans during the Civil War, and which Himmler visits that same month. She describes 'The terrible depressing ruins of the Alcázar, still with its pathetic remnants of furniture, old mattresses, stones piled before the windows, ceilings caved in.' For British people living abroad and hearing stories (often exaggerated by the Germans in Madrid) of the destruction at home wreaked by German aerial bombs, scenes like this must have been disturbing. Elisabeth would see these gaping buildings and imagine her friends living in fear of their own homes being reduced to dust.

*

Despite the risks, Elisabeth seems to love these journeys away from Madrid and the claustrophobia of the embassy, just as she used to relish her escapes to the countryside away from Peking. From her early diaries, it is clear that she is able to shift into new environments, she is prepared for challenging situations, and always seems to pack flapjack (which puzzles me until my mother explains it is not an oaty snack but a face-powder compact).

Elisabeth's early diaries also reveal an emotional reaction

to nature. She writes lyrically of the landscapes and environment, and paints what she sees. I get a sense that the young Elisabeth was happiest when away from the transplanted Britishness of life in the legations – when she was able to trek in remote mountains, camp in gorges and swim in the warm, milky waters of foreign seas. Whilst riding for miles across a Persian plain, she describes feeling as if she has slipped into a sort of coma, rocked by the horse's motion and awestruck by her surroundings. The American explorer Everett Ruess, who disappeared in 1934 after walking into the Utah desert, wrote about feeling stunned by the natural world and needing this energy: 'I am always being overwhelmed…I require it to sustain life.' Immersing herself in the landscape was an escape for Elisabeth, and a comfort; it was in her blood. Later, as Gerry's wife, it became a necessary counterpoint to her diplomatic duties.

Elisabeth's was an extraordinary existence: a curious mixture of maintaining a British way of life, and discovering the authentic essence of a place. Looking back over the places she lived we see an existence built on impermanence and marked by contrasts – she would travel for weeks on luxurious steamships, and then find herself in the back of a two-seater open bi-plane swooping over the paddy fields and dipping hills of Indonesia. I wonder how Elisabeth was affected by the constant flux and slip of her life.

Baudelaire wrote that 'Life is a hospital, in which every patient is possessed by the desire of changing his bed', and I sense in Elisabeth, even as a young woman, this feeling that she could be happy anywhere but where she is. An ambivalence permeates her diaries, an urge to settle and put down roots, but also a longing for thrills, for the adrenalin of movement. She writes this, back in 1937, whilst in China: 'There is something so unreal about life at the moment. It's all so abnormal. Well, perhaps after all this excitement one will be content to settle down somewhere and vegetate! Hard to imagine I fear... It's easier to keep alive (mentally) in places where one is perpetually stimulated by unusual sights and events – or even by unusual smells, as in China! It's also exercising to the mind to have to continually readjust it, as one moves from one type of life to another.'

In marrying Gerry, Elisabeth chose to replicate the rootlessness of her youth, a life of more upheavals and new beginnings. Many of the lists in her book are concerned with organising belongings in preparation for a move or journey, a means of dismantling her life and enabling it to be rebuilt somewhere else, usually at short notice.

*

In early 1941, after a difficult year in Spain and having waited for weeks to be told where they would be sent next, Gerry and Elisabeth are finally informed by the Foreign Office that they are to return to England. Elisabeth describes how, when she is told the news, she 'leapt back into bed and occupied myself happily with just thinking and making plans. What fun!' The act of making her lists and preparing for their return clearly gave her great pleasure – contradicting Major S. Leigh Hunt's derogatory claim, written in *Tropical Trials* in 1883, that 'The sudden and complete upset of old-world life, and the disturbance of long-existing association, produces in many women, a state of mental chaos, that utterly incapacitates them for making due and proper preparations for the contemplated journey.' Elisabeth's lists are thorough and meticulous, and she keeps them for future reference, neatly collected in the now wilting book, not scattered and discarded. I am reminded of Charles Darwin writing about his much-anticipated trip on *HMS Beagle*, in which he shows how he clearly relished the preparations: 'whenever I enjoy anything I always look forward to writing it down, either in my log book (which increases in bulk) or in a letter...Of course, I shall buy nothing till everything is settled; but I work all day long at my lists, putting in and striking out articles.'

The anticipation of travel is a powerful emotion. Making a list is a way of staving off anxiety about the unknown, and ensuring that we are fully prepared for our journey. I think of Felix Baumgartner, the Austrian skydiver, stepping out of his pod into space to fall twenty-four miles back down to Earth in 2012, and how the moments leading up to his incredible leap were dictated by a forty-item checklist narrated softly into his headset. There was a procedure, a framework, so that even though he was freefalling through the sky, the fall was anticipated and controlled by a list from far below. A list can be a matter of life and death. It can also hold clues to journeys and events that may otherwise remain a mystery, like the provisions list in the pocket of a corpse found clinging to the slopes of Mount Everest. The body's bones were bleached by the sun and ice, the head buried beneath the scree, the curves of the torso that gripped the mountain and the fluttering clothes pointing to this being a long-dead climber. It was, in fact, George Mallory. The list that had survived seventy-five years of mountain storms was an essential part of the evidence put forward by those who argue that Mallory had managed to reach the summit.

But a list can also prevent us from embracing possibilities that we cannot predict. We list-makers can veer into the realm of list-dependency, trying to frame potential experiences within the context of our lives at home. With a well-packed case and an itinerary of important things to see and do, we might absorb all the relevant cultural highlights, tick off the must-sees and write down recommendations of restaurants and hotels to pass on to other travellers, but there is less scope for spontaneity and the childlike wanderings of curiosity. A list should not be the end itself; it must not be a substitute for memories and experiences, but a framework for them.

For Elisabeth, I think the travel lists remind her of the possibility of escape. The lists are vital for her preparations, and she takes pride in her ability to organise her and Gerry's complicated lives, but there is a sense of freedom in whittling down the act of travel to its essentials. They become a spring-board for adventure, holding out the promise that sometime in the future she will be on the move and plunged once more into new surroundings. She will pack her flapjack, she will be prepared.

*

I can see elements of Elisabeth's restlessness in my mother – of wanting a real home yet being drawn to a life of fluidity.

Before moving to her present house, where she has lived for several years, my mother moved frequently and has a wanderlust that simmers close to the surface. Since she was diagnosed with incurable lung cancer, she has been travelling whenever possible, using her time to soak up as much adventure as she can. I recognise this impulse in myself, too. I spent most of my twenties flitting from job to job, career to non-career, place to place, with what I felt at the time to be a flighty charm. In reality, the cause of all this moving was not a devil-may-care spontaneity, but a sense of not belonging. I yearned for the family home that we had left when my parents separated; I longed for some stability, despite giving the appearance of embracing change. My life was giving me motion sickness.

I put my restlessness down to an ancestral itchiness of feet – I believed that somehow I had inherited a free-spirited love of moving, through my mother from my grandmother, but reading Elisabeth's book of lists has given me a new perspective on this aspect of my own life, as well as hers. Moving and travelling were an integral part of Elisabeth's childhood, and later her work as a diplomat's wife, but they also spoke to some deeper desire to be elsewhere. My own flight was from myself. And here's the thing we sometimes forget about travel: wherever we go, we take ourselves with us. That self may be altered in some way by the experience of journeying, and we can trick ourselves out of stuckness, but essentially we are still there, making lists and turning up in the mirror.

*

There is not much time to prepare and Gerry and Elisabeth's last days in Madrid are busy. Gerry cooks an omelette from what is left of their food stores, and they sit on the floor eating it, surrounded by empty cases waiting to be filled. Elisabeth packs and sorts their belongings, organises two farewell parties and sells their car and surplus clothes – all within two days. Her book of lists is a repository for both excitement and anxiety. It is different from her diaries, with their layers of narrative and memories laid down over the events she is recording – the lists are simpler, a place to hold rather than respond to emotions. Her packing lists give me the impression of being *with* Elisabeth as she packs, rather than reading a later account of events. I imagine her clutching the book, moving from one room to the other and ticking things off as she organises the end of one part of their life and the beginning of a new chapter.

Their journey home is not straightforward. Elisabeth is in the early stages of pregnancy and also suffering from flu; she is feeling fragile. Despite the care of Doctor Luque, a kind doctor who helped the Jewish refugees escape via the British embassy, she has had nausea and been exhausted for much of the first trimester. Now she must get herself and her unborn baby safely back across Europe. They travel first to Lisbon, where they have to wait for a plane home in what has become a hub for people travelling to Britain and the USA, often forced to wait weeks for a ship or plane out of Europe.

Whilst they wait for news of a flight, Gerry tries to nurse Elisabeth, on one occasion mistakenly rubbing her with *eau de cologne* instead of her medicated cream, which Elisabeth describes as 'a sticky error'. The delay is made more bearable by the profusion of food, in contrast to Madrid: hot rolls, huge pats of butter, honey, and eggs and bacon for breakfast. Eventually they are allocated a flight, and Gerry hands over an envelope to the pilot containing the details of their journey home (the exact routes are being varied to prevent enemy attacks). As they approach the English coast the windows of the plane are blacked out. Elisabeth cannot see much, but England looks different now: the roads are edged with barbed wire and concrete barriers, and trenches have been hollowed into fields. Spectral lines of rusted cars snarl across the landscape to prevent enemy planes from landing.

And how did the book of lists travel? Surely too precious to be sent with the other cargo, Elisabeth must have carried it with her on the plane burring above the Channel, and kept it close on all her other journeys. It becomes an even greater treasure when I realise where it has travelled. Just as Elisabeth's packing cases shift from one world to another, so her book of lists transports us to her wartime life back home.

5

Oxford

Norton's Things : Stored with Archer, Cowley & Co.
Pembroke Street,
Oxford.

1. Mahogany dressing-table with glass top.   ✗
2. +3.   "   loose-seat chairs.   •
4 +19   "   Book-case : (tall, two pieces; cupboard at   ✗
    bottom full of note-books, maps, photograph albums etc.)
5. +6. Cases of books.   ✗
7. Brown Trunk.   8.* Black Trunk   ✗✗
9. Mahogany 2-flap table. (Large; dining-room size).   •
✗10. Gramophone records   ••
11 - 17 - 18   Bed & mattress.   ✗
12. Mahogany oval table. (Smallish)   •
✗13. Deck-chair.   ••
14. Mirror for dressing-table.   ✗✗
15. Mahogany book & newspaper stand (low)   •
16. Small round table.   •
20, 21. Mahogany stuffed seat chairs   •
22. Linen basket   ✗

                                              P.T.O.

* Sent to Aunt Joyce, full of clothes.

MARCH 1941. AFTER GERRY AND ELISABETH RETURN FROM
Madrid, Gerry works in London and they look for a proper
home of their own nearby. German bombing raids rule out a
return to the city, so instead they decide on the countryside.
They stay with friends and relatives and in rented houses
while they hunt for a more permanent home. Elisabeth's
parents and sister are now stationed in Ankara in Turkey,
and her brother Norton is working at the Bodleian Library in
Oxford. He studied at Balliol College and is writing his book,
so it is a fitting place for him to take root.

The war makes it very difficult to travel, so Elisabeth and
Norton are somewhat isolated, with no way of knowing when
they will next see their parents or Alethea. Air raids, submarines and spies mean that travel must be purely essential
and planned in secret. In one letter their father writes to their
mother, when she is trying to get back to Turkey, 'Keep your
eye on the weather and especially on the wind blowing from
somewhere where I made a speech and met a parrot.' She was
left to decipher this cryptic message and find her way home.
Elizabeth does not remark upon her parents' absence in any

of her diaries; they are a family that is used to being far apart.
Yet Norton misses his father terribly.

Norton is a shadowy figure in our family history – in fact I
never knew he existed until I was in my teens. His life was not
exactly covered up, it was just that no one ever talked about
him. But in his letters to Elisabeth from when they were
young, I begin to get a sense of him. During their childhood,
the pair wrote to each other regularly and affectionately,
and their letters are spattered with terms of endearment
like 'darling', 'my little snowdrop', 'your little Topton' (a pet
name Elisabeth had for Norton). There is something cloying
about these phrases, a gushing, over-the-top exclusivity that
I feel Norton used almost territorially with Elisabeth. Their
correspondence paints a vivid picture of their relationship:
a fragile young man who was devoted (too devoted?) to his
sister and used her as a kind of portal through which he could
express his true self. She provided an emotional windbreak to
keep the complexities of the world at bay. He was often very
unkind about Alethea, making jokes about her appearance
and stupidity, mocking her for the fact that her tortoise died
because she fed it too much milk and bread, and even composing this amusing but violently gruesome recipe, written
when Norton was in his late teens:

> IV *Champignons Coeur d'Estomac*
> Pound Alethea to a pulp. Put pulp in pot. Take a
> barbell and some chocolate fudge & mash to a hash.
> Press, squeeze & squash. When it squelches, serve
> on toast. Turn to section on emetics, pp 2–36548.

In another scrapbook cutting from their childhood, Norton created an imagined obituary for Alethea stating that she 'died of obesity… Funeral will be held as soon as the body can be divided and suitable coffin constructed, all letters of congratulation to be addressed to her brother.' In this cutting, entitled 'Peeps into the Future – what we may expect', Norton and Elisabeth predict that he will die aged thirty-four on 26 August 1947, to be buried in his winter undies, and that she will die at her country castle entertaining her twenty grandchildren.

In fact, Alethea outlived both her siblings and was a kind, funny and rather lonely woman. At the age of eight, she contracted polio and was left with a leg that could not bend. In one letter Elisabeth refers to the ungainly manner in which Alethea got up off the ground, and her disability was doubtless a considerable source of sadness for Alethea and amusement for Norton. Alethea kept these letters and scrapbooks after Elisabeth's death, so she must have been aware of what had been written about her, but she always spoke of Elisabeth with fondness and adulation. She blamed her brother for the unkindnesses, but the teasing does show another, more waspish side to Elisabeth. It seems that Norton was deliberately belittling Alethea in order to strengthen the bond he had with Elisabeth, trying to protect their closeness against the threat of a young pretender. Playful taunting is commonplace between siblings and part of learning to cope with the tussles of the wider world, but in Norton's case it was more barbed than the usual rivalry.

*

Now that Elisabeth is back in England, Norton sees her fairly frequently, and she is planning to have her baby at a nursing home nearby in Oxford. Her parents will not be able to come back for the birth and she wants to be near family. It is a time when Elisabeth could renew her closeness to her brother, but the unborn baby is already competing for her attention and Norton himself seems distant. In March 1941, they spend a week together with relatives in Warwickshire, but on the journey home Norton seems increasingly anxious.

Oxford station is quiet that afternoon. Elisabeth watches her brother walk slowly along the platform as her train heaves gently away. She has always loved stations, with their sense of possibilities, the greetings and farewells, the ritual of buying tea and a newspaper before the train arrives. But something is amiss today. Norton has fretted most of the way back from Coventry, pushing impatiently past the crowds of soldiers crammed into the corridors, and constantly checking his luggage. He seems strangely agitated – he never likes saying goodbye to his beloved sister, but there is something else, a sadness etched across his brow, an emptiness in his eyes.

They have a vague arrangement to meet next month, when Elisabeth will return to Oxford for a visit. Norton steps away to find his car and drive into the town, with its buttery spires and leering gargoyles. He is so thin. He looks back, once, then turns, wraps his mackintosh protectively around himself and walks out of sight. Elisabeth sits back in her seat and exhales slowly, through her teeth. It is a relief to be alone again, to not have Norton's strained energy fizzing around her, but she is worried about him: he seemed better while they were away for the week together, relaxed even, but as the train drew nearer Oxford he had become increasingly jittery.

The train is taking her on to Sussex, where she will stay with friends. She is tired, her swollen belly pressing against her woollen coat. She cradles the baby, imagining it turning sleepily in the thick liquid of her womb, and then she takes out her knitting. The rhythmic click clack of her needles mirrors the sound and movement of the train. 'Look at what they've done,' Norton had said, staring at the devastation wrought by German air raids. 'We won't win you know. We'll soon be overrun with Nazis and that will be the end of it, darling. God knows what's happening to poor Mother and Father in Ankara. The town has probably fallen by now; they might even be dead. It really is too horrible.' As the journey wears on so Elisabeth's unease begins to congeal in her chest.

The guard passes and nods his hat to Elisabeth. A sharp kick followed by the still-surprising sensation of the small creature unfolding inside her stomach brings her back to the present. A faint wave of nausea washes over her, like in the early days. She pushes a curl off her face and decides to write to Norton as soon as she arrives in Sussex to make a definite plan to meet. But she will not see her brother again.

At some point that evening or early next morning, back in the flat in which he lives alone, Norton climbs into his empty bath wearing a pair of pyjamas, covers himself with an over-coat and swallows a lethal overdose of sleeping draught. His body remains undiscovered in its strange cast iron casket for several days. The shock of his death will ricochet through

Elisabeth for the rest of her life, the disbelief stinging like a slap each time she thinks of him.

*

The list at the beginning of this chapter looks at first glance like the other lists of furniture and possessions in Elisabeth's book of lists, but its matter-of-factness belies the sorrow at its root. It itemises things found in Norton's flat after his death. This must have been the hardest list Elisabeth ever had to make. It is written on a page previously headed 'List of China', the innocuous itemising of her household objects abruptly interrupted by her brother's suicide. The previous pages contain a 'Complete List of Linen', and lists of silver, plate, glass, all with headings in the same black capitals. But then the heading 'List of China' is crossed out by a single blue line and replaced with the words 'Details concerning opposite list'. Routine and everything Elisabeth knows is suspended here. The new heading feels like an intake of breath, a drawing-in of pain in order to reconfigure it into something practical. On the page opposite is the list of 'Norton's Things'.

The list is full of dots, emphatic crosses and smudges: the things Elisabeth is unable to control, the mess of life spilling onto the page, her emotions ebbing with the ink. Perhaps the crosses are merely to highlight the things still to be sorted. But a cross also symbolises a negative – it evokes finality. The list feels stilted and heavy. The crosses appear in only one other list in her book, written at a time when Elisabeth was suffering from postnatal depression, and I feel they must be significant. It is a catalogue of loss, Elisabeth bravely writing on, the words full of sadness, but also keeping her going. In contrast to the lists of items in her own home, there's an uncertainty here in her description of Norton's belongings – the detail she gives suggests that this might be the first time she's really looked at them, and may well be the last: 'Bookcase (tall, two pieces, cupboard at bottom full of note-books, maps, photo albums, etc.)...Mahogany oval table (smallish)'. Perhaps she feels she is intruding, that these intimate parts of his life were not meant to be examined in this way.

Norton's belongings are material remnants that speak, as a whisper, of a simple, unremarkable life, and not a particularly sentimental or happy one. The few mementos of travels with friends and photographs mentioned are in a cupboard, perhaps put away the night he died so they would not gaze upon him, or connect him to the reality of the world he was leaving behind. He seemed to be a solitary man who needed few belongings and even fewer people. Elisabeth lists an overcoat, perhaps the one in which he shrouded himself after climbing into the bath – was this thrown from his body when he was discovered, and later repacked, or did he choose a different coat? How do you choose the coat with which to cover yourself while you die? Did Norton want to be comforted by soft fabric and familiar smells, or wrap himself in something more solid to shield him from what was outside?

I am surprised to see that he owned three brooms, which seems unusual for a man living in a small flat, who certainly would have had domestic help. Perhaps this is merely evidence of a fastidious nature. The bath seems symbolic, a container for his body but also a way of controlling any unpleasant physical consequences of an overdose. The brooms, along with the way he chose to die, point to a concern with cleanliness and order. I feel sure Norton would have been a list-maker. I imagine the flat was left tidy and organised, everything in its place. But beneath this orderly surface there must have been anguish, and messy, uncontrollable sorrow.

The suitcase of clothes listed on the second page of Elisabeth's inventory of Norton's possessions was still packed, suggesting that he took the overdose soon after arriving home from the station, not bothering to unpack. I sense a clear-headed determination – it would have been so easy to distract himself and delay carrying out what he intended to do by sorting out his suitcase. But he was leaving that world behind, packed and stored in its case.

Lists can provide a scaffold on which we hang emotion while we repress it, or ignore it, or hold it up like a carpet and bash it until the dust flies. But this list of Norton's things also exposes an uncomfortable truth: that no matter how efficiently Elisabeth tried to prepare and organise the future, some things will always upset our plans. Death cannot be reduced, organised away or contained. Something will seep out.

*

My family's reluctance to talk about Norton and the mystery surrounding him is due, I suppose, to his sad end. Elisabeth's book of lists offers me an unexpected glimpse of Norton, and it sparks my curiosity. What drove him to suicide; who *was* he? I want to find this man who has been hidden within the layers of our family's story.

I feel sure that Elisabeth's letters and diaries will offer some clues about Norton's life and personality, about his loves and struggles. But he is strangely absent. There is the odd mention of him as a young man, and a comment on how an aunt had given Norton a car 'conditional on his "keeping a woman"!' (not a wife but a charlady, as it turns out, but the fact that this was a noteworthy comment stuck in my mind: it was unlikely that he would 'keep' any woman, perhaps?).

I find this picture cut out of a newspaper that shows the whole family at Waterloo station, waiting for their departure for China. I recognise the photograph, but the one I have seen does not have Norton in it. He stands to the left of his parents in this clipping, but in the other picture he is missing. Someone has cut him out. He is also glaringly absent from the contents of a mottled envelope marked 'Letters from the children 1919 onwards' (in red, crossed out, there are the words 'Papers kept to be read again April 1944' – these oddments must have been added after 1944, and therefore after Norton's death). Inside the envelope, Elisabeth's mother has

The family at Waterloo

stored a sweet note from Elisabeth to her father, dated 1921, in which she writes, in the curly, elaborate hand of a six-year-old: 'This is the first letter I have ever written, and I wanted it to be to you. Will you take me out again someday soon? Just you and I by ourselves. With much love and xxxxx Elisabeth.' The young Elisabeth clearly relished the time she spent with her father, and this note was cherished, kept for all his life. There are other letters from Elisabeth and Alethea (one of which is written on the back of a packing or shopping list, the list transformed into a missive, repurposed and reused), some caricature sketches of the family drawn by Elisabeth and, heartbreakingly, a copy of Elisabeth's funeral service. There is nothing from or about Norton.

Once more I feel a tingle of foreboding as I read their mother's report of Norton's condolence letter to his grand-mother on the death of his grandfather in 1939, in which he'd written: 'Grandpapa had a pleasanter death than is reserved for most of us.' Reading the letters between his parents in the weeks before his suicide is difficult – they are, of course, blindingly innocent of how the mundane details of which they write will soon suddenly be eclipsed by loss. I find myself imagining the shock and grief to come. I come across a telegram, sent by Elisabeth's parents to Alethea, who was travelling with friends in India when Norton killed himself. It merely reads: 'NORTON DIED SUDDENLY BURIAL MEREVALE DO NOT CHANGE PLANS.' It's hard to conceive how Alethea would have felt receiving this, miles away and with no means of finding out more. She is given the barest of details and must just carry on. It is a rather horrifying example of the stiff-upper-lipped self-control that people at that time – especially women – have to display, the overarching sense that they must constrain and resist any emotion or instinct in the interests of British foreign policy. Alethea kept the telegram in a small bundle of letters from Norton, fastened with some brown wool.

Neither of Norton's parents returns to England for the funeral. Of course, it would be very difficult for them to travel, but perhaps it was the very nature of Norton's death that also made it unlikely. I wonder if I should find out more about the grief experienced by parents of children who have killed themselves, but I can't, it feels too raw. It is, of course, a loss from which people never recover. I feel I would somehow be tempting fate and that I would later come to read my own words, as I am reading theirs, with the hideous clarity of hindsight after one of my own children dies. Even this sentence feels haunted. I am tangled up with these people and their stories, unclear where they end and I begin, my edges all blurry and uncertain. But I can't now look away.

Elisabeth was left to deal with the aftermath of Norton's death alone. I feel a surge of sympathy for her, preparing for the birth of her first child and suffering the enormous grief of losing her brother, while also having to organise his funeral and sort through the residue of his life. Pregnancy is often a time when emotions flood rather than trickle, smells are intensified, tears run frequently and unprompted, and happiness seems more urgent and technicolour. In this state, loss and grief seem to contradict the new life growing inside your belly – there is a reassurance that life continues, a hope for the future, but also a guilt that a life can be made so easily when an irreplaceable one has ended.

Norton's death must have been overwhelming for Elisabeth. She describes how she 'cried dreadfully – especially over the telegram from poor Nanny asking us to get some spring flowers for his grave'. It is interesting that it was a message from Nanny that particularly moved Elisabeth: Norton and Nanny had been very close, and he confided in her in a way he was not able to with his parents. Elisabeth here is acknowledging the loss that Nanny felt, as well as prompting my suspicion that Nanny's loss was simpler than that experienced by their parents.

*

I order the inquest papers relating to Norton's death. As far as I know, no one has read them, possibly not even his parents. The primary cause of his death is stated on his death certificate as broncho-pneumonia, caused by an overdose taken when the balance of his mind was affected. Chloral hydrate and bromide, the substances which were found in his body and in his flat, were commonly prescribed at the time to treat short-term insomnia, as a sedative and to treat 'acute melancholia'. Through his work at the Bodleian Library, Norton would have had the opportunity to research different methods of suicide, but it would have been widely known that these medications are fatal in large doses. They could also cause terrifying side-effects, like paranoia and hallucinations: the writer Evelyn Waugh (who was a friend of Elisabeth's mother's family) was known to take a mix of bromide, choral hydrate and crème de menthe in order to sleep, and he believed the drugs contributed to a mental breakdown in later life. There are no records of Norton experiencing such side-effects, however, and since he managed to save enough of his sleeping draught to administer a fatal dose, perhaps he rarely used it.

The drugs would, however, have had a definite effect on his body at the time of his death. As he died, Norton may have experienced hypothermia (hence the overcoat?), cardiac arrhythmias, respiratory failure, vomiting, nerve problems, hypertension, constriction of the pupils of the eye, and coma. Norton was right in that condolence letter: his grandfather had a far pleasanter death than his. During the autopsy, the coroner looked at the colour of Norton's skin; smelt his breathless mouth; noted the odours emitted when his stomach was cut open; examined the ridges in his belly; took fluid samples from his kidney, liver, intestine, blood, bile and urine; and noted the congestion in his brain. These are the visceral facts, the smells and gore of death, and I hope Elisabeth never found out any of these details.

Secrets have shrouded Norton's life for many years, but now I am stirring things up, poking around and exposing old wounds. For this I am sorry, but I can't stop – I need to know the truth, or whatever approximation of the truth I can get to. I am struck again by the sense that I am prying and that I have no right to know all this, particularly about someone so private. Yet the feeling that Norton has a right to be written back into the story is stronger than my misgivings.

*

As a child, my mother was told by someone (she can't remember who) that Norton had shot himself. Nanny told her that Norton had died in a lift. Perhaps Nanny was caught off guard by a question and this was the first thing that came into her head, or perhaps she just replaced the image of him dead in his bath with a less violent ending.

I begin to think that it is not just on account of Norton's death that he is so little spoken of, that there are other complicated forces keeping him in the background. There are family rumours about autism, an eating disorder and his sexuality. When I examine Elisabeth's list of his possessions, I am sure that some things have been left out. No letters are listed and there are none in the family papers, except those Norton wrote to his sister in his youth. Elisabeth noted that she took some 'oddments' and one attaché case, and a question enters my mind: did she have to hide something that she wouldn't wish anyone else to find? Elisabeth writes in her diary of Norton's pink dressing gown, a flamboyant article of clothing that contrasts with the rather plain items on her list. I want to know why the dressing gown is not here with his other possessions. What is excluded from a list can be as significant as what is included. With Norton, it seems that it is the omissions that speak loudest. What Elisabeth wanted to remember is the brother who is encoded in her list; what is left out is another, more complex part of their story.

After speaking to family members and reading Norton's letters, it becomes apparent that he may have been gay. At a time when this was not only socially unacceptable but also illegal (until the passing of the Sexual Offences Act of 1967),

Norton would have had to keep this hidden.

From what I have learned of him, it seems likely that this secret would have horrified him and caused him great torment. Perhaps the pressure of having to deny such a major aspect of his identity contributed to his reaching such a point of despair that he felt dying was a better option than living.

It is clear from Elisabeth's diaries and letters that Norton didn't 'fit in' and was never comfortable in his skin. He wrote many letters to Elisabeth in a gushing, feminine tone, his writing peppered with comments about his 'little complexion' and passages like this: 'the state of your poor blossom's nerves, my dear I'm definitely a delicate flower, any shock too upsetting, my dear I wasn't made for frights'. He finished one letter, 'Well life isn't all powder and undies, as Shakespeare said and I suppose one <u>must</u> do a <u>spot</u> of work every now and then, just to show what we girls are capable of…'

Elisabeth's family developed a strategy of ignoring the issue that they were unable to address. Homosexuality was better not mentioned; that made it easier to believe it didn't exist. This is a common approach in families at this time, where a 'don't ask, don't tell' policy was deemed the only way forward. I recall some research into why children cover only their eyes when they are trying to hide. They know that their head and bodies can be seen, but they don't imagine these physical things as being their 'self'; it is their eyes that contain themselves, and therefore the eyes that must be hidden. Elisabeth's family were all hiding their eyes in the belief that nothing else would be seen. From what I have read in Norton's own words, in diary entries written by Elisabeth, and in remarks about conflict with their father, it seems likely that it was perfectly apparent that Norton was gay, but it was never publicly discussed or acknowledged.

I also find some hints that Norton was struggling not only with his sexuality but with his body:

> I was weighed, 8st 12oz!
> …as some fragrant bishop said only the other
> day, if you can't control your cubic capacity you
> can't control your conduct which I think is so
> right…Of course darling, I rather despise all
> food, I merely eat what I'm given.

Evidence presented by Norton's doctor at the inquest describes how Norton would regularly appear at the surgery to weigh himself, suggesting a fixation with his weight. The doctor notes that Norton was 'a curiously introspective and unresponsive patient who seemed very determined to muddle along by himself in his own flat'.

It is hard not to look at photographs of this troubled young man through the prism of these snippets of information. In his sideways eyes and curling lips, I see evidence of sensitivity, loneliness, alienation, but maybe that is because this is what I am looking for.

How do we reconstruct a life without superimposing these retrospective values upon an individual? I don't think we can, but I also don't think it matters, really – what I am doing is patching things together in order to make sense of the pieces that I have. It is impossible not to project our

Norton

own hopes and expectations onto anyone with whom we have a connection, dead or alive, and I realise that in writing Norton's story, I am hoping to make my family's narrative clearer, to give it definition and unpuzzle the mysteries. It takes me closer to finding Elisabeth.

I read the inquest papers on a drizzly morning on a train to Eastbourne. A chill slides over me. The seventeen bottles of prescription sleeping draught that were found in his bathroom show that Norton had planned his death for some time. He collected one bottle every two weeks from the chemist over a period of ten months, stashing them away, waiting until the time came to end his life. I think back to Elisabeth's concerns about Norton's state of mind, and reports at the inquest that during their stay at their uncle's house the week before his death, his behaviour had been normal. But it seems that as he came closer to the time when he had to say goodbye to Elisabeth, he became more agitated. I think he had made his peace with the world, knowing what he was going to do, yet still felt a dread at the reality of their last farewell. I also can't help wondering about the significance of the date on which he chose to commit suicide: 26 March, his father's birthday. Was there some kind of subconscious 'adverse reaction' to this date, a sense of failure to be the son his father wanted, or a desire to punish him in some way?

There is a suicide note. No one has mentioned this to me before, ever. He addressed the note to his father and writes: 'I am shortly going to take as much of my accumulated dose of sleeping draught as I can manage and hope that it will prove lethal. You know the reasons, food shortages and increasing debility and weariness – unlikeliness of us winning the war etc. etc.' The brusqueness and offhand reasons for his action appear unsatisfying somehow. Many people in Britain during the war suffered from constant exhaustion and lethargy, but for someone so concerned with their weight, Norton's citation of food shortages seems contradictory. The 'etc. etc.' may be a reflection of his weariness, but still, I am curious about Norton's reaction to the war.

Norton was not conscripted at the time of his death – probably because he was medically unfit having had a bout of tuberculosis. Regardless of his health, he would have dreaded the prospect of being called up (Elisabeth writes after his death that he had been depressed by 'the possibility of being called up for work on some war effort'), and clearly would have loathed being in a military environment even if not directly involved in the fighting. After recounting an episode where he fainted during a military drill at school, he writes, 'I am nature's civilian.' Norton eventually persuaded his father to have him excused from these parades – something that may have been difficult for a man brought up to conform and do one's duty, but which shows concern for his son's welfare, and perhaps even a desire to protect him from discovery? The echoes of these humiliations may have fed into Norton's feelings about the war, connecting the soldiers he sees in the streets and the talk of war with the shame and horror of school military drills.

The stigma of being of 'LMF' (Low Moral Fibre) attached to any man who showed fear or weakness in the RAF during the war, and with such an unbending and unsympathetic code of ethics, the military would have seemed an anathema to Norton. The early part of the last century was not an easy time for those who were unable to conform to the stereotype of the fearless warrior, nor to be gay (if there ever has been such a time).

During the First World War, men who were openly gay were regarded as depraved and deemed detrimental to the war effort, and an implicit connection was made between being gay and being a traitor. The 1920s saw a more liberal, bohemian culture emerge out of the senseless slaughter of the war. As F. Scott Fitzgerald writes, 'Here was a new generation...grown up to find all Gods dead, all wars fought, and all faiths in man shaken.' Oxford, where Norton was to study and live, was known as a place of sexual liberation and freedom. Gay bars flourished in many cities, but amongst the mainstream population, homosexuality was largely still regarded as sinful and perverted.

Norton's own cousin Bill, whom he visited frequently and with whose family he stayed in the week before his death, had first-hand experience of this hostility towards gay men. Bill's uncle, the Seventh Earl of Beauchamp (said to be the inspiration for Evelyn Waugh's Lord Marchmain), was known by seemingly everyone but his wife to have a penchant for young footmen. When in 1930 his vengeful brother-in-law threatened to use Beauchamp's homosexuality to publicly shame and expose him, the earl was faced with the choice, as he saw it, of suicide or exile. He chose the latter. The shocked king is reported to have said, 'I thought men like that shot themselves.'

In 1936, just a few years before Norton's death, twenty-nine men from Altrincham, near Manchester, were prosecuted for homosexual practices, and during the trial, the prosecutor claimed the seriousness of the charges was second only to murder. The trial was reported in the national press in veiled language. Terms such as 'improper conduct' were used rather than explicit references to sexual activity, and the 'evidence' on which the case against the men was built consisted of letters, lipstick, slippers, flowers, the use of nicknames like 'Queen Mother', and the signatures on hotel registers where the men stayed. Such a massive and public scandal would surely not have escaped Norton, who, if he were gay, would have further cause to repress his feelings. The following year, two men committed suicide together, and in 1938, two ex-soldiers were imprisoned after being discovered to be living together as lovers. That same year a Dorset doctor recommended that special gas chambers be built next to the courts in order to get rid of those found guilty of 'perversion'.

Later in 1941, the year Norton died, the MP Paul Latham was imprisoned for indecency and attempted suicide. He had driven his motorbike into a tree when evidence of his 'improper behaviour' with other men was discovered.

Against this background of intense scrutiny and public condemnation of love between same-sex partners, I imagine Norton hiding himself, perhaps unwilling to accept what he knew to be true. It would have been difficult to have any meaningful friendships when he was unable to openly be himself, and the shift in tone of his letters to Elisabeth as he grew up, from gushingly camp to restrained mundanity, was possibly a result not just of increasing maturity but of his awareness of the socially unacceptable nature of his very being. Was this the reason for the lack of later letters amongst all the family documents – was he withdrawing and hiding, writing less in order to protect himself?

The years of the Second World War did provide greater opportunities for closer relationships between men, as troops were posted away from home and the binding moral codes of their families. Intimate friendships between servicemen were tolerated, but sex between men was still punishable by court martial and resulted in dismissal or imprisonment if discovered within the armed forces. As the war progressed there developed a more pragmatic 'no questions asked' approach, because as many men as possible were needed to fight.

For those left behind, the heightened sense of danger and imminent death, along with nightly blackouts, led to a growing underground queer scene, particularly in the bars and galleries of London. With the later witch hunts of the 1950s and 1960s, there was a spike in suicides by gay men, including Alan Turing, the mathematician and breaker of the Enigma code. Turing killed himself in 1954 following his conviction for gross indecency and enforced castration via hormone therapy. After the end of the war, there was an increase in the number of arrests for sexual deviancy and an introspective focus on the family and domestic life. Dresses or effeminate clothing (Norton's pink dressing gown?) were used as evidence in the trials of men suspected of being gay, and overtly camp men were at risk of public derision. The possibility of being outed would have been appalling to Norton. And this fear, along with the feeling that, by not joining up in some capacity, he was dodging his duty, a principle that had underpinned his childhood, must have contributed to his self-loathing and melancholy.

The war alone doesn't seem reason enough for suicide. There was, doubtless, a unique harshness to life at that time, an odd combination of dread and dreariness. Fear of what was to come had certainly played a part in Elisabeth's earlier depression, and Norton would have felt very worried about his family caught up in the war so far away. Yet he was used to living away from them, and the fact that he mentions in his suicide note that he had been planning his death for some time (possibly before the impact of the war really took hold) reinforces my belief that he was struggling with inner demons that he could not disclose. His assertion that his father 'knows the reasons' implies that his family must have been aware of his struggles, that there are no surprises. His reasons seem vague in isolation, but taken as part of a general feeling of melancholy and depression, they have a greater significance.

I wonder if time moved impossibly slowly for Norton, the days stretching into each other with little to distinguish them and no apparent way out. I remember a sentence by Olivia Laing: 'the perfect weight of loneliness, the sensation of wrongness, the agitation around stigma and judgement and visibility…the familiar, excruciating sense of lack'. Norton's own words conjure something similar – a great, grey blanket of loneliness and despair that is slowly smothering him to death. Perhaps life just didn't hold enough for him; perhaps he simply didn't want to go on living any more.

Another thought floats into my head as I trawl through Norton's letters to Elisabeth: that his sense of isolation may have been compounded by the fact that she was pregnant at the time of his death. He may have already felt he had been replaced as her closest *confidant* when she married Gerry, but perhaps this unfurling new life represented an unbearable shift in her affections and focus. Is it possible that in the act of suicide the perpetrator embodies or enacts wrongs that they feel have been done to them? Did Norton abandon his sister because he felt impossibly angry with her for abandoning him?

But possibly – probably – these are all the wrong questions. Perhaps there is never one 'rational' explanation or reason for suicide; it is instead a culmination of intangible helplessness and emotions that are impossible to pin down. The assumption of reason negates the apparent irrationality of killing oneself, an act that is wrapped in a cloud of despair and regret so thick that we may never see through it. As the actor and writer Stephen Fry explains: 'There is no "why", it's not the right question. There's no reason. If there were a reason for it, you could reason someone out of it, and you could tell them why they shouldn't take their own life.'

In his suicide note, Norton writes that he had decided to kill himself previously, but left such a long and emotional farewell letter that he talked himself out of it. It is hard to imagine this earlier letter, and what he wrote that would be compelling enough to write himself back from the brink. The actual suicide note is intentionally dispassionate and disconnected – he knew that if he explained himself fully, he would open up an invisible line of communication with his family, and that he couldn't bear. Perhaps this is connected to the still-packed suitcase, a trap of procrastination and nostalgia that he refused to fall into. Instead he focuses on the practicalities: the bath, the overcoat. For a terrible moment, I am reminded of my mother's recent meeting with an undertaker to plan her funeral and choose a coffin (wicker – cardboard being environmentally unsound, apparently). She needs to know that the chaos of life has been made manageable for those she will leave behind. The circumstances are very different, but the feeling must be the same: controlling what is in our power to control in the face of the ultimate unknown.

*

So how did Elisabeth cope with the death of her brother? How did her parents deal with the sorrow, shame and loss? Mostly, with silence. The contents of Norton's suicide note confirm one reason for their taciturnity about his death: it would have been politically damaging to the war effort for an ambassador's son to mention the 'unlikeliness of us winning', and his father would not have wanted to comment on this publicly. I discover that references to Norton were removed from his father's entry in *Who's Who*, and Elisabeth writes in her diary that the letters her parents wrote just weeks after his death didn't mention Norton and were 'very quick…which is a blessing…So the worst is over for them.'

This reveals a poignant naivety in Elisabeth, but also the way that death was dealt with in her time: she thinks that the initial shock of grief must be the hardest part of losing someone, and that once this passes, normal life can resume. She doesn't yet know how much the loss of her brother will haunt her or how his death will cause an unmentionable hole in the family. The fact that Norton was so little discussed from then on reveals a kind of visible blankness, a sense that the world will never be quite the same, yet this absence cannot be acknowledged. It must have been hard to grieve in this atmosphere. In her diary, there is a description of the last time she saw Norton, and at first I think it must have been written *after* his death, because the words seem to hang in a portentous cloud: she mentions their 'final words' and describes how 'as the train left I saw him making off for the car again, looking very tall and thin, and swathed in a mackintosh'. But the quotidian details and recounting of ordinary conversation in

Elisabeth's diary entry must have been written in real time – it seems too strange and unnecessary to add these after such a traumatic event. Instead, perhaps Elisabeth's description is backlit with a sense of foreboding, as though she somehow picked up on the fact that *he* knew it would be the last time she would see him.

She had clearly been concerned about Norton, describing him as depressed, 'fussed and exhausted' by their journey, but also wrote that he had seemed on good form during the week they had spent together. He had spoken of how, after the war, he wanted to move to Crete, to read and write and be 'quite independent'. I read this as meaning he wanted to be alone, cut off, quiet. He had asked Elisabeth to darn all his socks, which seems an implausible request for someone planning to kill himself only a few days later. But maybe the darning of socks was a metaphorical way of tying up loose ends before his death. Norton wanted Elisabeth to perform one last act of care and love for him; he wanted everything to be in order before he departed.

I shake off a shameful and unreasonable prickle of disappointment in Norton: others were having a far harder war than he was. Why did he choose to take his own life now, at a time when Elisabeth needed him? I come across a letter written by Mrs Kathleen Hicks, wife of the Bishop of Lincoln, published in *The Times* on 27 April 1941 following Virginia Woolf's death (she drowned after plunging into the icy River Ouse on 28 March, two days after Norton died). The letter offers an insight into the response many people may have had to Norton's death at the time:

Sir, I read in your issue of Sunday last that the
coroner at the inquest of Mrs Virginia Woolf
said she was 'undoubtedly much more sensitive
than most people to the general beastliness of
things happening in the world today'... If he
really did say this, he belittles those who are...
carrying on unselfishly for the sake of others.

This charge, that Woolf committed suicide because of
the war, so upset and angered her husband, Leonard, that he
felt compelled to publicly correct the assertion: 'She took her
life, not because she could not "carry on", but because she felt
she was going mad again and would not this time recover.'
The belief that her suicide was due to unpatriotic cowardice
reflects a wider disavowal of the anguish that Woolf, and by
the same token Norton, suffered. No doubt Norton's parents
feared he too would be tainted by this view (especially if his
suicide note ever came to light), and bring more shame on
the family. The Foreign Office requested that the inquest into
Norton's death be held *in camera* due to the sensitive nature of
Norton's father's work. In other words: cover it up.

I imagine that Elisabeth must have been anxious as she
prepared for the funeral. As the sole member of Norton's
immediate family in attendance, she would have to endure
any criticism alone. In the event, Elisabeth notes that one aunt
had declaimed his suicide as 'wicked and selfish', but most
people present seem to have been understanding and kind.

*

I decide to visit the apartment block in which Norton died. I park outside on a gravelly half-moon, gazing with a shiver of unease at the red-brick 1930s' building. Two women are tending some hanging baskets, and it looks like a nice place to live. I ring up an elderly, helpful member of the street's residents' association, who confirms that I have the right building and I find myself stumbling over my words. I'm not sure what I am hoping to find. Some sense of Norton, I suppose, of the view from his window, of the tree he would have turned his back on as its branches began to bud with spring leaves; a way into his head. But it feels macabre, and I am worried about knocking on a stranger's door and saying, 'Hello. My great-uncle killed himself in your bath. Could I come in and have a look around?' so I end up driving away. Elisabeth didn't have the privilege of escaping. Someone had to go round that flat, noting down his belongings, dismantling his life.

In her diary following the funeral, she writes that she has had to collect Norton's car, but 'thankfully' hasn't gone into his flat; however, this horror was merely postponed. I am not sure how long after Norton's death Elisabeth eventually makes the trip, but she takes the book of lists with her. Gripping its solid binding she has a purpose, she mustn't dwell on the reasons why, but be systematic, thorough and organised. I imagine her picking up each small object, feeling a connection with Norton through the spine of a book, sweeping the wood of his desk with a hand as if stroking his hair. Maybe his smell lingers somewhere in the flat. Did she go into the bathroom and stare at the bath, or did she avoid it, walking past, shutting the door? Was anyone with her, or did she have to do this alone?

Norton's death must have been almost unbearable to Elisabeth, but the routine act of making a list of what he left behind must, I think, have brought some kind of order in the wake of something in which she could find no reason. In the depths of sorrow, a simple list can be a support while the ground cleaves beneath us. The act of fixing the details of life on paper enables the gathering-in of loss, the reshaping of incomprehension into meaning and action. After losing a loved one, the bereaved walk a wire, balancing between getting on with life and keeping those we have lost close. I think of Philippe Petit walking his tightrope between the Twin Towers in New York in 1974: each delicate, breathtaking step moving him towards safety but also away from the security of where he started. There is a point in the middle where he is suspended, equidistant from both points. Whilst this may have been the point where Petit felt most free, where he wanted to linger and play, it is perhaps the most difficult place for the bereaved, moving from the deceased being the centre of their world to a new way of being without them, a point in which time stretches ahead and leaves the other behind. The wire, here, takes a different form – a list of possessions – connecting Elisabeth to Norton yet helping her walk away. At some point she arrives, in her grief, at a new place of being, but the wire remains.

*

Norton's death is the only one that features directly in Elisabeth's book, but it is because of Elisabeth's own death that I am piecing together her story. Her end is where I start from.

As I read the list of Norton's things, I feel Elisabeth struggling to contain her grief, but I am also aware of other griefs, barely contained and pushing at the edges. For me, Elisabeth's life has always been framed by the fact that she died young and left my mother motherless. Now, with my mother's diagnosis, there is a new layer to this story: I see her loss, but I also see my own. And I am scared that there is also another layer: the loss my children might face in the future. My mother had two primary cancers and recovered, but a new tumour has developed and is killing her. Both her parents died from it. I am struck square-on by the fear that cancer is coming for me too.

After my mother's diagnosis, my abstract interpretations of how lists enable us to cope with death are suddenly nose-diving into the gaping hole of my own mortality as I wrestle with the hitherto unacknowledged belief that I will be next in line for this cancer that has knotted itself into my mother's chest. There are plenty of lists that are supposed to help us navigate as she slips slowly from us: lists of emergency contacts, lists of questions to ask consultants, lists of who is coming to help and when, lists of instructions for her funeral. Elisabeth's story seems more real in the light of my mother's lists, more potent. It is strange to think both women could have been making very similar lists as the ends of their lives come closer. Death feels like a clammy breath on my neck, and I sense myself drawing in, preparing for a duel with cancer that I may need to fight in the future.

I am not alone in this fear of cancer. It is the most demonised illness of our time, despite not being the biggest killer. We often see a diagnosis of cancer as leading inevitably to a slow, painful death, despite many people recovering or living satisfactorily alongside their illness. Perhaps it is its randomness that gives cancer its power: the healthiest of people can succumb, it affects young and old, some people go into remission whilst others die. As humans, we crave an ordered universe but cancer's unpredictability disrupts all certainties, and so the list-makers among us try to impose our own sense of order.

This awareness is painful – I imagine the suffering awaiting my mother – but I am getting closer to the curious, fragile cord on which this book is balancing: our need to control, and the impact of something so *uncontrollable* as death. Perhaps this pernicious, silent horror of death is at the root of my quest for Elisabeth. In piecing her life together, am I trying to defeat some inevitable foe? Is my fascination with Elisabeth's book of lists part of a struggle to come to terms with my mother's impending death, with my own mortality, and the effect my death would have on my children? Lists are a buffer against the void, and this book is perhaps mine.

Freud believed that when we lose an object or a person, we begin a process of mourning in which we eventually find them within ourselves. I didn't really lose Elisabeth, I just lost the *chance* of her. What I do have is my mother, bravely enduring chemotherapy and its ravaging side effects, planning the next month but not much further ahead, living as well and as fully as she is able. I imagine the other lists my mother must be making in her head in preparation for what is to come. I try to imagine what it is like to face down your own death, to be preparing for and trying to make sense of a future that isn't your future. For the last few years my family and I have been living in a strange suspension, knowing that my mother is dying, and watching with awe and befuddlement as she embraces the end of her life. She is going on cruises, holding meetings to discuss dying, organising her house and belongings. She is ready to die. But we are not ready for her to go, not even slightly, and although I am so pleased that she is living these last months without regrets, I have many.

I regret that she may not hold this book; that I choke back so many words as I watch her stepping gradually backwards away from me; that I haven't asked the right questions; that I can't show her how much she is loved. I resent the God in whose hands she so readily places herself, wishing I could believe (as she does) that she will be reunited with Elisabeth and Gerry and that there is some higher purpose for what is happening. People often say what a blessing it is to have this forewarning of her death, to make peace with it gently, but it feels like we are constantly cowering under the shadow of a catastrophic storm that could strike at any moment. She has been 'well' for such an unexpectedly long time that Death has slyly sidled to the edges of the room, keeping its eyes on us as it retreats and bides its time in the corner.

6

Surrey

Things for Samuel - Susan

Sister's list :— stores +
(Ordered from Treasure Cot):—

2 Hair pillows ✓	**Baby clothes etc.**
6 Pillow slips ✓	✗ Bath (borrowed)
2 Mackintosh sheets ✓	Scales "
Hot water bottle ✓	Cradle "
Safety pins ✗	Notes basket "
Vinolia baby-soap ✗	Pram (present: £8:8:0)
Taylors Cumdirtie powder	Cot mattress etc ???
	✗ Baby ribbon

Soft sponge ✗, waterproof apron ✗ ~~travelling apron~~ Mackie

(Ordered from A. & N. stores).—

1 Box zinc & starch powder (1 to 3)	**2** Small shawls.
1 Pure Vaseline	1 Big Shetland Shawl
1 glycerin + borax	✗ 3 doz. Harington Squares
1 3" crêpe bandage	2 Doz. Turkish towel "
1 surgical spirit	4 Silk & wool vests
1 Dett. "	6 Childproof vests (borrowed)
2 lbs. medicated wool	? 6 long lawn dresses (G.P.Y)
1 " " " in drum	4 " Viyella "
2 lbs. gamgee tissue	2 Flannel & 2 lawn petticoats
Dettol + tube Dettol cream	Endless coats, boots, pilches etc
1 lb. Lint. 3 Doz. S.Ts	✗ Bottle & Teat

AFTER NORTON'S DEATH, A PREGNANT ELISABETH SPENDS a nomadic few weeks travelling between various friends and relatives, floating like the feathery seed head of a dandelion, unable to take root. I wonder if she is simply incapable of staying still. Finally, though, she begins to find her centre of gravity at Rock Cottage, their new home near Godalming in Surrey. It is only a temporary rental, but she quickly settles into a routine, as Gerry commutes to London and she keeps house.

She writes: 'I've never lived in the country before, though always imagined I should like it – and now I <u>know</u> I do… It's a simple, pleasant life here.' The contrast to the whirl of diplomatic life is stark: here her days are spent making beds, tidying away the breakfast, going back to bed and writing her diary once Gerry has left for work, listening to the wireless, having lunch, reading, sewing and helping with the washing on a Tuesday. No cocktail parties, no breakneck escapes down mountains running from the secret police. Despite the hardships of wartime England, they seem happy. It is a time of non-travel, of being settled.

Gerry at 8 p.m.

Each morning, Gerry takes the bus up to the Foreign Office, sometimes having to stay overnight when air raids or work prevent him from returning home. When he does get away, he stops at the pub to buy drink to take home for the evening, and strolls down the lane to the cottage. Elisabeth seems to be enjoying the quiet of this part of her life. She writes of long walks and tea with women in the village, and of practising nursery rhymes in preparation for becoming a mother. It is precious, this simple happiness.

*

The list entitled 'Things for Samuel-Susan' is a page-long account of things Elisabeth had to buy (or borrow) in preparation for the birth of her first child (named Samuel-Susan whilst *in utero*). Reading this list took me straight back to the feelings I had about my own first baby's imminent birth. I knew that the shape of our world would be altered irrevocably by the birth of our child, so alongside the excitement, there was a subtle sense of loss – a grief for a relationship or family unit that would never be the same. I felt anxious that everything should be in place, that the essential objects that the baby would first meet in the outside world were ready. There was an intense pleasure in seeing a row of tiny white babygros swinging on the washing line, as I imagined the body that would slide into the clothes and into our life.

The year in which Elisabeth's baby is born (1941) is a complicated one for her: the war is going badly, she has recently lost her brother, she has no permanent home and her parents are living abroad. But her baby list doesn't look much different from one a woman might write today – albeit without the plethora of temperature-measuring/ sound-monitoring/ guilt-allaying gadgets with which we have to wrestle. She ordered most of the equipment and clothing from Treasure Cot, a large department store equivalent to Mothercare. I find one of their advertisements from 1931, which encapsulates this combination of a new mother's anxiety and anticipation. The advertisement shows an image of a (rather scarily large and old-looking) baby above the words:

> Are you expecting me? Do you know what I
> shall want? Have you everything ready? Every
> tiniest thing you need for the great event
> is here at Treasure Cot. Guidance, too, for

the inexperienced, given with such kindly
understanding. Love can do no more for a baby
than prepare for his arrival here.

I discover several bizarre contraptions that have been
marketed to new mothers since the start of the century: a
baby holder for use on public transport, with a lid to close
when the baby is crying; a kidnap detector light; a full-body
gas mask complete with a rubber lung to be pumped by the
person holding the baby; a UV light for branding the baby's
initials onto their skin, to avoid hospital mix-ups; a baby
walker constructed from wooden planks that strap a parent's
and the baby's legs together; and a metal rod with a seat belt
to hold the baby in place in the bath. I am relieved not to
see any of these items on Elisabeth's list, though I can't help
feeling that some of them might have appealed to Gerry, who
loved ingenious inventions and improvised DIY devices. (He
once had a car with a radiator that wasn't working, so he and
his father attached a toilet to the roof so that it would flush
water into the engine when the chain was pulled.)

Elisabeth's list of things for the baby shows how seriously
she is taking her new role, and below another list ('choc. Bath
essence. Sat: sherry & books, haddock, fruit'), in pencil, she
has noted the names of parenting guidebooks that she wants
to get: one is *The Motherhood Book for the Expectant Mother and
Baby's First Years* and another by Dr John Gibbens, *The Care
of Young Babies*. I wonder what expectations she and Gerry
had for Samuel-Susan. If he turned out to be a boy, he would
eventually inherit a title and ancestral home, and he would

carry the weight of the family line. What if her son or daughter showed an interest in diplomacy; would she encourage a different profession or a different marriage? Did Elisabeth want a more stable life for her children than she had had?

Whatever the thoughts and anxieties that must have been whirling through Elisabeth's mind as she wrote her 'Things for Samuel-Susan' list, she could not possibly have foreseen the orphaning of their children. Something in this list of prenatal preparations gives me a sudden and vertiginous sadness, an urge to jump into the page, to bury myself somehow in the inky lines and warn her of what lies ahead. I imagine a tiny Borrower-like version of myself standing inside the book of lists, wrenching the words off the page as if lifting a heavy cable, and moving them into a different pattern, as though that could create a different future. I feel like a voyeur, privy to information of which the subject is oblivious, and I have to haul myself back into the present, and to see Elisabeth's baby list on its own terms: as a hopeful precursor for motherhood.

For this list does hold hope, as so many lists do – hope that things can be better or different if only we make a plan. The brain craves completion, and a list provides a solution. In this way, a list can be seen as a letter to a future self. We have to visualise a self that is well, happy, functioning, a self free from shame, a self performing its tasks efficiently and happily. Hope, no longer merely perching in the soul, is externalised into a list. There is a list in Anne Frank's diary in which she notes the things she will buy on an imaginary shopping spree in a pretend world where the family is living freely and happily. It is practical, with costs, and not extravagant. She wants to buy an ice-skating outfit (oh, how she must long to glide, to swoosh through the cold air, cooped up as she is in her tiny refuge), handbags and a make-up case. The list is hope poured onto paper.

Hope moves us on and when it dies we stagnate; a list can pull us onward, out of our torpor and into a new life, a new self, in which the world makes more sense and we know what we are doing there. There is a ritualistic quality to Elisabeth's list book, as if the lists are a kind of prayer.

*

April 1941. Elisabeth sits up in bed, propped on plump pillows, writing her diary. From the window, she can see the wet tops of the trees being buffeted by a cuckoo wind, and the garden spattered with the yellows of daffodils and primroses, as if the sun has blasted shards of itself down to Earth. Gerry has just left, walking quickly down the narrow lane to the bus stop. Elisabeth sinks deeper into the pillows, pulling the top of the dressing gown he bought her in London (designed to withstand the ravages of baby vomit) over her chest. The air smells faintly of bacon and rain. Thoughts scud across her forehead: *How good it is to be finally settled in one place for a while! What's that French nursery rhyme Mother used to sing, something beginning with 'Coucou'? When will the order from Treasure Cot arrive? Perhaps I will cancel it altogether and ask cousin Veronica to get the last few bits for the baby. Now that clothes are to be rationed it's a good thing I laid in a store of baby things. I'll check that list again, to be sure.*

She is enveloped in the feathery quilt of domesticity, sheltering from the worst of the horrors of war, getting by, turning inward. Time has become stretched here, as she waits for her baby to be born, knowing that soon she will be too busy to write in her diaries. She is both impatient to meet the baby and aware that she must relish these last few quiet weeks. Her pen scratches across the page. She recalls her early diaries, the violent landscapes and constant sense of possibilities and adventure, and sighs gently. It is a sigh composed of regret and relief, and it hangs in the air.

Outside, the quiet is broken by the triumphant crowing from a neighbour's hen that accompanies a newly laid egg. They will have hens, soon, once they have found a permanent home. And for now, they have Rock Cottage.

*

Reading Elisabeth's book of lists, and plotting its journey as I map out her life, leads me on a journey of my own, around the lanes of Surrey rather than somewhere exotic. I decide to try to find Rock Cottage, the house where Elisabeth spent the final months of her pregnancy and where she seemed to find a new kind of contentment. I want to walk the landscape where she was happy, when life was good, so that I can carry it with me when I uncover the dark places. On my way back from visiting my mother and stepfather after one of her bouts of chemotherapy, I take a detour down the A3. I know the name of the village and of the house, but that's all. Perhaps a cursory glance at an Ordnance Survey map would have been useful, but this is not a well-planned journey.

Rock Cottage

I find the village and park at the end of the lane. It is sunny and quiet and charming. A woman in jodhpurs walks behind a large, tangly dog and throws me a breezy 'Hallo!' I walk and walk, and I feel as if Elisabeth is walking beside me. It is a weird sensation – thrilling, but it also somehow makes me feel self-conscious, as though I have allowed myself to become too bound up in someone else's story.

The lane becomes rougher, the surface scarred with potholes and deep ruts. The leafy trees form a canopy overhead, giving me the impression of being in a tunnel. The dappling light recedes and the fields alongside cut away steeply, leaving me with the sense of walking too far into gloom. I keep going, scurrying now, ridiculously clutching one of Elisabeth's photo albums so I can cross-check the houses against the pictures.

The lane peters out and I am forced to give up. I pass what I think must have been the farm I saw in a photograph, and I hold the picture up to compare it. But I cannot find Rock Cottage. I hear someone mixing cement in a farmyard and wonder if they could help, but the thrum of the machine drowns out my hesitant calls of 'Hello?' I am running out of time.

Disappointed, I head back to my car. I am woefully ill-equipped for this trip, with barely any petrol and just a packet of salt-and-vinegar crisps to sustain me for the day, and I have failed to find the cottage, just as I failed to see Norton's flat. I am not sure what I hoped to find by visiting these places. It is unrealistic to expect a location to unlock a door to the past and let you simply step through into someone else's world. And yet, just by treading in Elisabeth's footsteps, by walking with her in these quiet spaces – she would have walked down the street where Norton lived, she would have known this lane, this farm – I do feel closer to her, and I also feel a deeper sense of belonging to a story that is bigger than my own. There is a motion to these parallel journeys I am following: the book of lists' voyage around the world, mine to find Elisabeth, my mother's into death. There is a tidal flow, we are together yet distinct, and I am caught in its current. As long as Elisabeth is making her lists, as long as I am immersed in her world, my mother is still here.

*

A delivery arrives at Rock Cottage, marking the crossover from diplomatic to domestic life: Elisabeth and Gerry's luggage from Madrid. She writes, 'Busy as a bee with all our luggage that has just arrived from Spain. Most of it is battered, and some of the suitcases have been well soused in sea-water, and are also full of soot. It's a bore having nowhere permanent to unpack in…However, I suppose we're lucky to get them at all – they dodged the U-boats.' This description brings her packing lists to life, painting an image of her suitcases bucking in a briny hold while the ship darts between enemy submarines.

Elisabeth and Gerry are looking for a more permanent home for after the baby is born, and after much deliberation they settle on another rented house, a place called Warren Farm, near Guildford, Surrey. Elisabeth is keen to make a nest for her new family. In July 1941, she goes to Oxford to stay with friends at New College, so that she can be near the nursing home where she is to have the baby. Just a few months ago, they had planned for Gerry to stay with Norton when visiting Elisabeth in Oxford, and his absence must have been deeply felt.

Her pregnancy has been straightforward and she is happy with the nurse they have found to look after her and the baby for the first few weeks (whom Elisabeth refers to as the 'Sister'): she is kind and quiet – not at all starchy and brisk. The birth begins dramatically. Elisabeth wakes in the night with contractions but the phone lines are down and she can't ring for a taxi to take her to the nursing home. An undergraduate offers her his motorbike, but Elisabeth feels this would be unsuitable. The waves of contractions are buckling her body. After two and a half hours a car is sent and she gets to the nursing home just in time. The baby – Samuel George –

Elisabeth and Samuel

is nearly born in the car. (Many years later, Samuel will deliver his own grandson in a car on the way to a hospital.)

After the birth, Elisabeth and Samuel stay for two weeks in the nursing home and settle into the routine: the baby is wheeled in at 6 a.m. after spending the night in the nursery with thirty other newborns, Elisabeth breakfasts at 7.30 a.m. and then spends the next two hours in a frenzy of feeding Samuel and getting both him and herself bathed, then a lull when she writes letters, eats lunch and naps until the afternoon feeds. The first time Samuel really yells, Elisabeth is terrified and bursts into tears herself.

After the nursing home, Elisabeth, Samuel and the Sister go to stay at Parham, in Sussex, the home of Elisabeth's dear friend (and cousin) Veronica. This house will provide shelter, relief and safety for Elisabeth in the years to come. What should have been a happy time in fact becomes a dark period for Elisabeth. No matter how much we read or how well we remember all the paraphernalia, nothing can really prepare us for the upheaval and shock of becoming a parent. For many women, this shift from being an individual to being a mother is smooth and joyful, but for some, including Elisabeth, juggling sleep deprivation, hormonal chaos, surges of emotion and the weight of being responsible for a tiny being can be overwhelming. With a birth comes a death – the loss of one-self and the replacement of one identity with another. This can cause an existential crisis that manifests itself in feelings of despair, inertia and hopelessness. Women also absorb the social constructions of motherhood, internalising these roles and experiencing acute grief when they fail (who wouldn't fail?) to live up to the idealised version of the 'mother'.

For Elisabeth, this was further complicated by being a diplomat's wife, having to shift between different societal perceptions of 'success': whilst abroad, she was judged on how many cocktail parties she threw and how charming she was; now she measures her own success by how well she can feed and care for her baby. Elisabeth and Samuel return from Parham and the family move to Warren Farm, their new rented house near Tillingbourne in Surrey, where she experiences the beginnings of a savage depression. She feels terrible, cries all the time and worries about everything. The Sister reassures her that this is perfectly normal, that it is just the 'baby blues' and it will soon clear up.

Over the next few days, Elisabeth feels sick and cannot eat. She worries constantly about the baby suffering if she doesn't eat, and feels guilty about not being able to help Gerry set up the house. In her diary, she describes how she began 'to feel more and more desperate. It rained & Samuel seemed to be crying more than usual, & I got worried, & we couldn't get his nappies dry, & Patterson [the housekeeper] complained about the stove & couldn't keep the water hot. O dear – I did so want to get it all going properly.' The cadence of this sentence is frenzied, just as thoughts run into each other and one worry cartwheels into another. Her world is spinning out of control.

Knowing how unhappy she was there, the list of things for Warren Farm makes me shudder. It feels cold – a desperate attempt to be positive and practical. I can sense the effort Elisabeth was making to set up home, and the list contains markings and numbers that don't appear elsewhere. It holds her deep inhalation as she mustered the energy to pick up a pen; the writing seems heavy, laboured, in thick ink strokes. Her sadness leaks from the page.

Just three days after moving in, feeling despair at the Sister leaving and utterly overwhelmed by having sole responsibility for the new baby, Elisabeth wakes Gerry in the middle of a sleepless night and begs him, through exhausted sobs, to get her out of there. She goes back to Parham and, with support and help, her appetite returns. But she can't shake the feeling of hopelessness: 'I hope I feel different soon, I can't stand this unreasonable depression, wanting to cry, missing

Sister, & thinking about Warren Farm – and worrying about just <u>everything</u>.'

Slowly, Elisabeth begins to feel better. The weather improves and she is more confident looking after Samuel. After the first disastrous attempt at making up his bottle – all the sterilizing, straining and boiling, all the tears – she can now do it properly. The household in Sussex is a mixture of her cousins, staff and various refugees who have been sent from London along with their teacher. They are busy picking and bottling fruit and drying apple rings. Things seem more normal and the depression recedes. But when she goes back to Warren Farm to check on things, Elisabeth feels 'that terrible despair creeping over me again'. It is as though the house has become a receptacle for her depression, holding the sorrow in its walls, the furniture screaming, 'You are doing it all wrong! You are a failure!' Gerry and Elisabeth decide to move out. The next list in her book is 'Things taken from Warren Farm' and I feel a feel a rush of relief, just as she must have felt when writing it and leaving that house behind.

7

Little Oaks

Egg Register (Six pullets, hatched Oct. 1941, delivered to Little Oaks on March 15°)

~~March 28°~~

Date	No. of Eggs	
Sat. 28°	1	Aunt Lettice (white)
24	1	(brown) 1½ oz.
25°	2	Brown, white
31st March	2	" "
1st April	2	", Brown 2¼ oz. double-yolked
2nd	1	
3rd	2	
Weeks Total	11	

April 4°	 2	(one more hen lay)	April 11°	 2	
5°	 3	2	12	 1	
6°	 2		13	 3	
7°	. . . . . (3 soft shelled on the floor!)		14	 4	
8°	 4		15	 3	
9°	 3		16	 4	
10	 3		17	 5	
Weeks Total	20*		Weeks Total	22*	

* but counting 3 bad shots.

* not counting almost daily soft-shelled ones on the floor.

IT IS AGREED AT THE START OF 1942 THAT ELISABETH AND Gerry will move to a house called Little Oaks, in Kingswood Warren, Surrey, which they will share with Gerry's sister Joan, who is pregnant, and her husband Robert. There is also a housekeeper, and a bad-tempered cook-cum-maid named Dora. Elisabeth and Joan share the chores not done by the servants, and take charge of the garden, where they plan to grow vegetables to keep the house 'safe from starvation', and to keep twelve hens, rabbits and a goat. Elisabeth is excited, and finally seems to be in good health. She turns to her book of lists to source food, seeds and essentials for this new home, once again pouring her energy into the preparations. The house is rented furnished and is a manageable size, with four bedrooms (including a maid's room), a dressing room for the men, and a larder and scullery off the kitchen (which has a gas cooker). There is a good-sized garden, leading down to the oak trees that give the house its name.

Elisabeth has Samuel to look after and a household to manage, but she isn't required to perform her previous role of diplomatic hostess. This is a period of pause, of recovery

Little Oaks

(from the loss of her brother, from postnatal depression), of withdrawal from the static-buzz of public life. In these moments of stillness, when our minds meander and time seems more nebulous, sometimes the mundane details of life take on a new significance. She wants to make a success of being a suburban homemaker and, as ever, uses her lists as a way to guide and map out these next months and years, to mark time and the moments within it.

Elisabeth is in her element: 'We've settled in here very happily, and really it seems <u>exactly</u> what we want. I enjoy it all thoroughly, with lots and lots to do – but all amusing and pleasant things. Semi-suburban life seems to suit me. There is something essentially amusing about having neighbours living in houses called 'Sunset' and 'Nocturne', and popping down to the village shop with the other housewives. Not what I'd like for ever, but a pleasant contrast to diplomatic life abroad.'

*

Elisabeth's 'Egg Register' list spans four pages and contains a running total of 897 eggs, sometimes logged next to the name of the hen and a description of the egg. She carefully notes the number of eggs, any hens that are broody or moulting, and any soft-shelled eggs she finds. At the top of the page is a rusty paper clip which bears the tarnish of age, crumbling and russet, standing to attention but with nothing to contain. When I remove it, there is an imprint which seems like a ghostly shadow of Elisabeth, just as these lists are. I turn it over in my palm and wonder what important piece of paper was clamped between the pages, padding out the book of lists, changing its surface and leaving only this corroded reflection. Or perhaps it was used as a page marker during all those months of recording her hens' laying patterns.

With all the other household chores she has to do, it is something of a surprise that Elisabeth would choose to make a list as ongoing and detailed as the Egg Register. As a chicken-keeper myself, I am in awe of her dedication to noting not only the number of eggs, but also which hen laid them. My morning foray into the chicken coop is usually a hurried affair, sliding in the sludge whilst stopping the hens escaping. I doubt I could have enough wits about me to notice which eggs came from which hens every day, let alone record them. But I can relate to her sense of wonder and thankfulness at finding an egg nestling neatly amongst the sawdust, knowing that no matter what else happens that day there will be a wholesome, fresh meal for my children. For Elisabeth, writing her list at a time when food is scarce, a cracked egg would have represented a greater waste, and finding a double-yolker amongst the day's eggs a real joy. I love the fact that she records the successful laying of eggs at a time when she has just become a mother.

When the first of the six pullets lays an egg Elisabeth writes: 'An active day – but culminating in the breath-taking event of the FIRST EGG! I could hardly believe my eyes when I spotted it, as I gave a perfunctory glance into the nest-boxes, after feeding the hens.' The list here is evidence of her success at self-sufficiency; every egg that is logged is proof that they are making this life work. Simple and unglamorous though it may be, it is *hers*. The Egg Register is a statement of gratitude and affirmation.

*

Elisabeth's Egg Register speaks as much of wartime England as it does of her life at Little Oaks. Across the country, eggs are rationed to one per adult per week, and people are encouraged to keep their own hens by the provision of chicken feed coupons in exchange for egg rations. Chicken-keepers must use whatever materials they have to hand to construct coops and runs, as proper building materials are hard to find – Gerry and Elisabeth make their chicken run from an old tennis net. Hens are fed a mixture of bran and mashed, boiled left-overs, and although it often takes an entire morning to prepare the feed (Elisabeth even describes mincing raw fish scraps), plenty of eggs could be provided by just a few hens, as her Egg Register demonstrates.

Wartime necessitated organisation and frugality on the domestic front. Women of all classes had to learn to make do with what was available. It was a time of ingenuity and improvisation, but also of drawing upon wisdom carried down through generations. There was a wealth of published advice available in the form of manuals and recipe books, of which perhaps the most well-known is Mrs Beeton's *Book of Household Management* (1861). Mrs Beeton's manual was regularly updated and later editions were aimed at a growing readership of middle-class women who were having to take on tasks that had previously been performed by swathes of servants. The book included tips for household economy on a low income, menu-planning and the use of leftovers. Mrs Beeton's belief that the mistress of the house was like an army commander would have resonated with readers during a time of war.

Many women would have received advice and tips from their mothers, but I can find no record that Elisabeth's mother offered any guidance on keeping house, although I am sure she would have schooled her daughter in how to be an efficient embassy wife (by example, if not explicitly). In any case, her own experience of running a home with an extensive staff in various far-flung embassies would have been a world apart from the challenges Elisabeth now faced in wartime Britain. Instead, Elisabeth had her book of lists. And just as she had found her own method for fulfilling her duties as a newly-wed, and a diplomat's wife, so too she found a way to run her life under rationing.

At the Mass Observation Archive I discover a box of journals kept by a woman I will call D__, one for each year, between 1929 and 1977. These notebooks begin as detailed household accounts, but to my joy I discover a small black book, about the size of a playing card, full of lists just like Elisabeth's. There is even a list of eggs laid by D__'s hens.

From the information I can glean, D__ was a housewife of modest income, living first in Enfield and then moving to Somerset, where she raised her children. She was a fierce budgeter, keeping a record of income and expenditure, as well as Christmas presents, to-do lists, and even the minute details of a dead rabbit called Jacqueline. The outgoings and income mostly tallied exactly, but occasionally she would have to borrow an aspirin or a stamp from a friend. She kept accounts of expenditure on food, stamps, paper, leather, windows, chemists, cottons, laundry, socks, toys, homework, collars, sticky tape, calendars and Woolworths. It is all there, nearly fifty years of a life broken down into each tiny component part. In spite of their social differences, I feel sure D__ and Elisabeth would have got on.

One contemporary of Elisabeth's wrote, in a diary from 1947, of having to choose between essentials and food: 'Spending half my weekly money on food and trying to get blankets, zips and other materials as well as extra coke and coal has nearly floored me. I have gone on strike, I have decided to cut out some of the food.'

In the back of her book of lists, I find that Elisabeth has stuck in a recipe for carrot marmalade. My son and I make it for his History homework assignment on World War II. While not quite a family recipe, I feel glad to have made something that Elisabeth made too, and it was easy to imagine that the smells swirling through our kitchen might have filled the kitchen at Little Oaks too: a pot of plain vegetables from her garden transformed into a sticky-sweet breakfast treat. There are other recipes in the book, and one funny diary entry recounting a, presumably dictated, Chinese recipe for beef tea: 'S'pose 2 man chow puttee ½ lb beef chop very small first time. Puttee beef two cups water saucepan. Downstairs have got other saucepan. Water boil, topside steam. Puttee salt-pepper. After take away beef altogether very nice. Piece lemon.'

*

Next to the Egg Register in Elisabeth's list book is an inventory of stores from which to source various goods that were hard to come by, notes on how to plant sixteen garlic (2 inches deep, 6 inches apart) and the title of a poultry-keeping leaflet produced by the Ministry of Agriculture. As more ships are needed for fighting and attacks on supply vessels increase, imports of food dwindle, and the government is pushing the notion of a 'home front' in order to galvanise the civilian population into producing their own food. The 'Dig for Victory' campaign encourages gardeners to dig up their lawns, plant vegetables and keep livestock, whilst public spaces like parks and the gardens of large houses are converted into allotments. Vegetable patches appear in the most unlikely places, and factory yards and urban spaces are also used to house pigs or grow potatoes. There is a shift in perception from gardens being places of beauty and sanctuary to having a more utilitarian function as the national larder.

As author and gardener Ursula Buchan describes, as well as providing food, there is also a psychological benefit to all this digging and planting: as people work the land they are reinforcing their bond with the country that is being fought for. There has long been an implicit connection between our history and the earth we stand on, a way of literally ground-ing the abstract idea of 'nationhood' and belonging. The soil becomes more than just mud; it represents the history of a nation, of ancient kings, of warriors and farmers, of pioneer-ing settlers. The wartime government is keen to reinforce this morale-boosting aspect of self-sufficiency, conjoining patriotic duty with working the land. This is the beginning of Elisabeth's love of gardening, which grows out of an exter-nally imposed imperative but blooms into a lifelong desire to combine beauty and functionality in the outdoors. It is a way for her to feel she is contributing to the war work, to feel useful and independent.

The careful process of clearing weeds, planting seeds, watering the soil and watching tiny shoots appear also represents the victory of new life in the face of the mass destruction and horrors of international warfare. In the crops of potatoes, sprouts, onions, carrots, leeks, beans, peas, cauliflowers, beetroot, cabbage, redcurrants, marrows, black-currants, parsnips and turnips, in the production of compost and experiments with fertilisers, Elisabeth (along with families and communities across the country) draws strength and solace from the natural world. The poet Alice Oswald has written of this close connection with nature through working the land, writing that 'Raking…is a more mobile, more many-sided way of knowing a place than just looking… you can hear right into the non-human world, it's as if you and the trees had found a meeting point in the sound of the rake.'

Elisabeth embraces this new life, enjoying, for a while at least, the simple and quotidian jobs of tending her garden, keeping house and feeding her family. Her world is smaller, but it is the first time Elisabeth has had such complete domestic control, and perhaps she feels empowered by this too. It is often said that the war brought about dramatic changes in the role of women – allowing them for the first time to take jobs outside the home that had traditionally been the preserve of their fathers, brothers and husbands. Many leave the home to work in munitions factories or in the armed forces, or join the Women's Land Army. Some join the Women's Voluntary Service and do important work distributing food and clothing, and running the National Savings Scheme. But these roles are performed on top of their domestic jobs, meaning that they also have to cope with the usual demands of housekeeping and cooking. Given that just buying food can involve long waits in several queues, and there is no proper childcare provision, life becomes extremely challenging for many women.

The war imposes contradictory demands: women should be feminine and nurturing, but also work and join the war effort. These ambiguities are reflected in the clothes they wear – red lipstick and neat dresses, tidily curled hair, legs bronzed with a gravy tan; overalls, headscarves, work boots. Clothes and fabric were subject to rationing for a significant part of Elisabeth's life, and for her and her contemporaries this posed additional challenges. Women felt the need to 'keep up appearances', to look attractive for the menfolk away fighting but also to bolster their nerves and soothe anxiety during the deeply stressful wartime years. For some, the financial independence that came from going out to work, perhaps for the first time, meant the freedom to spend their money on make-up and hairdressers. There are accounts in the Mass Observation Archive of how working-class women in Stepney in 1940 are dressed; most of those under fifty wear heavy foundation, lipstick and have their hair permed. Straight hair is seen as a sign of poverty and women attend hair salons as often as finances allow to keep their Marcel, Steam or Eugene waves looking tidy. Financial constraints often mean choosing between a hair-do or the pictures. These women are asserting their rights to self-expression, yet also conforming to societal norms.

It is easy to oversimplify or romanticise life on the home front. It is not all ruddy-faced land girls rolling up their dungarees and merrily toiling away. In reality most people do not grow their own food, let alone become self-sufficient. The long hard years of living with such real and omnipresent danger take their toll across the nation. Like many women, Elisabeth is left at home with her children during the terrifying air raids, having to keep her nerve despite feeling so helpless. Families are separated, homes are destroyed, loved ones killed or injured, food and clothing are scarce, people are exhausted and everywhere is enveloped in the seemingly endless darkness of the blackout.

Elisabeth was initially buoyed up by her efforts as a wartime housewife. If she can survive incendiaries and handwashing endless nappies and mincing fish scraps and not knowing whether Gerry will make it home at the end of each day, then she can surely survive anything. Yet for Elisabeth, as for many women, the grind of scrimping, mending, working, looking after children, enduring bombing raids and fearing for the lives of her loved ones is sometimes overwhelming. Nothing is one thing or another, life flips and slides, the focus shifting constantly according to the eyes we bring to a picture.

Many women deal with the fear and dangers of wartime in a way they may not have previously believed they were capable of. Elisabeth, who always seems to keep a cool head in times of crisis (like the frantic journey to Shanghai after her father was injured, or drinking a gin fizz during an air raid in Gibraltar), again has to draw on her inner resilience. In November 1943, she gives birth to her second son, Charles, who joins Samuel (and Joan's baby, Theo) in the Little Oaks household. The presence of these young children makes the dangers of war seem more intense and frightening. One afternoon a bomb drops near the house and a large piece of twisted metal lands in the garden in the place where the babies usually sleep in their prams. Elisabeth describes the attack in her diary:

Joan and I were both in the kitchen, getting tea
ready, and for once there wasn't an alert on. We
heard some of our planes going over – and I said
to Joan 'What a relief to hear the RAF and not
the flying-bombs, for a change.' Just at that very
moment there was a terrible roaring overhead,
and one of the brutes dived out of thick clouds –
I heard it circling over the house, the engine still
running, but it was obviously about to crash,
and then I threw myself on the floor and felt my
hair rise on end in terror. There was the most
tremendous bang, and glass fell in and the whole
house rocked…But after a fraction of a second
one realised it was not a direct hit…Was shaking
like a leaf, and Joan and I tore round to see what
the damage had been. A good many windows had
gone, a door was dislocated from its hinges, half
the tiles were off one side of the roof, and upstairs
the wall in Theo's room appeared to have 'moved',
and a huge crack in one corner had appeared.

No one is hurt, but the metal debris marks the pervasive
dangers of war, and it is as if something menacing and deadly
has been flung into their midst. The month after the bomb,
a plane is shot down nearby, demolishing half a house at the
end of their garden, just before a children's party was about
to get underway. The plane circled over Elisabeth's house
before plunging to the ground, its engines still running. She
becomes 'more nervous of these things, and several times put

S & C to sleep under the sideboard in a corner of the hall far away from all windows'.

For Elisabeth, this is a period in which she sets down roots whilst things fall from the sky and the world is torn apart. Her diaries and list book have fewer entries for this period because she simply doesn't have the time or energy to write. One diary entry spans two pages and retrospectively outlines a typical day's work, and she describes how 'every now and then the work "got on top of me" & I felt absolutely dead. Which annoyed me, as so many people have to do as much & more all their lives.' Elisabeth seems vulnerable here, and I am proud of how she copes with little domestic help (she fires Dora after a confrontation over lettuces) in circumstances very different from those in which she was brought up. The act of writing out these seemingly endless chores over two pages is an acknowledgement of the slow, incremental work of living.

And so she goes on tending her vegetables, counting her eggs.

*

Although Elisabeth is often exhausted by the domestic work, and by the strain of the war, the time at Little Oaks is a period of relative calm. But at the end of 1943, after Charles is born, the darkness descends again. Elisabeth is once more engulfed by postnatal depression.

After leaving the nursing home with her baby, Elisabeth goes to stay at her grandmother's flat in London. In London, and away from her family, Elisabeth wakes that first night with horror, experiencing 'those terrible symptoms I'd had after S & that had caused such months of misery. I felt very sick, very worried, & very tired…A horrible struggle against the depression and feeling of mental turmoil and worry.' She battles on, believing that if she goes back to Little Oaks she will be so busy with the children and her chores that she might be able to stave off the waves of hopelessness and have no time to worry. But depression doesn't work like this.

It is hard to read Elisabeth's descriptions of her feelings at this time – she seems so vulnerable and desperate, and Gerry is clearly trying hard to help her. She writes: 'Looking back on today I think it was one of the "maddest" & more unpleasant I ever spent…The things about the house that always depress me seemed impossible to overlook, & loomed larger than ever. I really nearly walked out of the house because I felt I just could not stand it. I keep crying, feel utterly exhausted, but above all it's the turmoil in my head that is impossible to bear…After dinner I was so worn out that I more or less collapsed I felt so mad.'

Elisabeth's doctor advises her to wean the baby and to go back to Parham to rest. She is given some pills to 'straighten out' her glands, which are deemed to be causing her problems. The pills don't make any difference so she is put on a course of three sets of different pills, again aimed at treating 'gland trouble'. But this time even being cossetted and cared for by her cousins in Sussex doesn't seem to ease her mind. She describes what happened: 'Veronica & I now refer to these two horrible days as "Suicide Sunday" and "Punishment Monday". My "madness" seemed to reach a climax. & I really did feel as if I might go clear off my head…I <u>knew</u> I should be a raving lunatic if I could not get someone to talk to me & reason with me & calm me. After 24 hours of indecision I eventually followed Cousin A [Alicia] into the chicken-run, braced myself together, told her I felt quite mad, & asked her to come and talk to me.'

This helps a bit, and after a day she feels less mad, although she still feels like crying all the time and is completely exhausted. At this point Elisabeth's mother flies to England to see Elisabeth, which is an indication of how serious her condition is. Elisabeth is nervous about this meeting, worried that it might be too strained and disappointing, but it goes well. Her mother reports back to her father in a letter that 'I saw E's doctor on Wednesday; he is worried about her, but has given her 3 separate medicines, & hopes that they & Parham will put her right. He hopes a month will do it, but I have made her promise to stay on as long as Alicia thinks necessary…V's theory is that the very bad fit of gloom she had last week was the climax, & that, having unburdened herself of all her worries & foreboding to V. she will now be rather more rid of them, & that now it is only a question of building herself up… She seemed very bobbish & cheerful this morning & I personally have found her quite normal, though she is <u>terribly</u> thin & drawn.'

Elisabeth's parents also have another problem to deal with at this time. A spy working as her father's valet is discovered to have been selling information to the Germans, including documents about significant events and Allied plans. The scandal shakes Elisabeth's parents, not just because of the very public humiliation and shame of being duped, but also because this man, known as Cicero, had worked very closely with them. It is said that he would sing through the bathroom door to Elisabeth's father whilst he bathed, and photograph secret documents as he sang. Her father comes out of the scandal looking naïve at best, and incompetent at worst. It is difficult for her parents to recover their professional pride after this, and the affair may have distracted them from the seriousness of Elisabeth's depression back in England.

I get a sense here also of a general, wider ignorance of mental health problems, as well as a desire for things to resolve themselves quickly and with minimal fuss. It is clear that Elisabeth was making a huge effort to seem normal for her mother, perhaps unable to reveal her true vulnerability and brokenness. I also wonder whether Elisabeth's mother saw frightening echoes of Norton here – the thinness, the desolation, the madness?

*

Another list, folded into a box of letters and written in pencil on two pages of paper:

Things That Worry Me

My determination to find everything wrong

My inability to face anything

The trouble I give everyone

I don't <u>want</u> to do anything [this line is darker, more emphatic – anger perhaps?]

Isn't it my own fault, & aren't I letting it all
become an attitude of mind?

My horror of L.O. [Little Oaks] but _____ [?]
of the effort of making any change – I might be
equally unreasonable about any other place

I like being here [Parham] more than anywhere
else. But I feel it's not fair on G if I can't spend
a certain amt. of time with him. He's been so
uncomplaining all this time

Money comes into it all the time

Not quite sure what I <u>do</u> want, that is really
attainable, that fits in a) with G b) possibility of
going abroad

Anyway <u>why</u> should <u>I</u> have what I want?

I seem to have no control over my mind or
moods

Gerry's feelings – he mustn't feel this is all his
fault

Don't know how to begin describing the things
that upset me, but I can't stand these 'fits' much
longer. I let myself be 'persuaded' and talked to,
& then go right back again afterwards

I see in this list confusion, sadness, self-disgust, an attempt
to make sense of what she is feeling, a lack of resolution. It
is her torment exposed, and it makes for painful reading.
It also shows how Elisabeth used lists, and her diaries, to

try to contain these overwhelming emotions. The staccato sentences and emphatic underlining in this list read like an automatic writing exercise, an attempt to get her thoughts, unedited, out of her head and onto paper. She is trying to diffuse her fears, and reassemble the fragments of a broken self. Lists may perform a different function here – rather than the open-ended spaciousness of a diary page, a list is clearly defined, limited. There is little room for thoughts to grow, and perhaps when a mind is turbulent and wretched, these simple inventories stop our emotions from running unfettered. Elisabeth, as in her list of Things That Worry Me, needs this outlet to rationalise the furious mess inside her head and the world beyond, what Oliver Sacks referred to as the 'buzzing, blooming chaos'.

Interestingly, this list is not written in the book of lists but on a scrap of paper. This may have been because it was all that was to hand, but I suspect she saw this as a shameful list, a record of not coping, in direct contrast with the ordered experiences and objects she contains within the book of lists. Yet her response is the same: write out the worries and keep writing until they are bled dry.

I am reminded of a passage in Jeanette Winterson's *Why Be Happy When You Can Be Normal?* in which a librarian explains the comfort she gets from the Dewey decimal system: "'Whenever I am troubled,' said the librarian, "I think about the Dewey decimal system…Then I understand that trouble is just something that has been filed in the wrong place.'" Elisabeth's lists are her filing system for her troubles, and her joys, triumphs and boredom.

Dutiful, self-controlled, conscientious: these are the characteristics of a list-maker, and the very characteristics that were eluding Elisabeth during her depressions. Perhaps her list of worries is a means of reconnecting with this part of her, of quieting her wild mind and trying to find a way back to herself. She is taking responsibility for creating the order she lives by. Of course, none of this abstract thought was relevant to Elisabeth, convulsed with despair and fear, feeling she is losing her mind.

While Elisabeth suffered periods of depression throughout her life, it was the bouts of postnatal depression that were the most severe. As we see in the Sister's dismissal of her troubles after Samuel's birth as the 'baby blues', this was a condition that was not recognised, let alone treated properly. This speaks to the wider issue of attitudes towards women's mental health at the time. Traditionally, mental illness in women had been dismissed as 'hysteria' (a purely female condition, thought to stem from the womb). A study in 1914 found that one woman with a brain tumour had been certified, her tumour overlooked; another supposedly insane woman actually had concussion and a fractured vertebra.

However, attitudes towards mental illness more generally were changing during the 1940s and there was an emerging focus on the physical causes. New treatments were being developed that targeted the brain directly, including electroconvulsive therapy, lobotomy and leucotomy. There was also a growing emphasis on less invasive ways of altering brain chemistry through psychopharmacology, with drugs such as benzadrine sulphate and methedrine, which became known as 'Mother's Little Helper'. These medicines were designed to sedate rather than cure the patient. Mental disorders like anxiety and neuroses (the word 'depression' was rarely used and only a small number of people were actually diagnosed with this as an illness) were seen as biological diseases, and medication was seen as the only effective treatment.

In the 1940s there was a popular theory that thyroid dysfunction caused mental health problems (Elisabeth's 'gland trouble'?), and I remember this being mentioned by my mother, and also in accounts of Elisabeth's final illness. One of the most frequently prescribed medications was 'Dr Williams' Pink Pills', which were essentially an iron tonic, marketed for the treatment of clinical depression, anaemia, poor appetite, nervous headaches and lack of energy. I find a reference to pink pills in Elisabeth's diary and feel a wave of sympathy for her: tangled in the horrors of postnatal depression she is offered merely an iron supplement.

In recent decades, Freudian and Jungian psychology had also gained popularity and the 'talking treatments' were now offered alongside medication. Elisabeth had seen a psychiatrist in London before her marriage, and perhaps her list of worries reveals a frustration that talking her troubles over and letting herself be 'persuaded' just doesn't seem to be working. There is a sense that Elisabeth blames herself for her illness ('Isn't it my own fault, & aren't I letting it all become an attitude of mind?'), perhaps reflecting the more widespread wartime pull-yourself-together mentality, which we saw in relation to Norton, too. And now she has two small children to look after, compounding her shame and frustration with herself that she just isn't managing.

At a time when there are so many terrible fatalities and casualties on the front line, the impact on the women back home, who are coping with rationing, war work and bombing raids, tends to be overlooked. Women are supposed to be holding together not just their families but, by implication, society, and they are suffering. The dominant message is one of duty and 'sacrifice', which must contribute greatly to the feelings of guilt and inadequacy experienced by women like Elisabeth who can't cope. There are around nine million full-time housewives in wartime Britain. It is a tough time to be a mother. As author Virginia Nicholson notes, pregnant women are given extra meat, eggs and orange juice concentrate and have priority in ration queues, but they sometimes have to give birth in air-raid shelters, their husbands hundreds of miles away. Some women struggle to produce milk and even miscarry due to malnutrition or stress. Mothers with older children have to endure the pain of separation if those children are evacuated. There is little time for sympathy for someone like Elisabeth, whose mind is thickening with a syrupy, slithering depression.

Elisabeth's wartime lists, like the Egg Register and Things That Worry Me, are even more significant as the physical landscape around her is being irrevocably changed – bombed, dug up, pierced with barbed wire, requisitioned. For Elisabeth, it became even more crucial to gain a sense of control over the things in her life that mirrored the chaos of the wider world. I imagine the air rent with sirens and thick with smoke, the mantle of fear that must have descended, the adrenaline permanently coursing through the veins; and a woman picking up her pen and her trusted list book, organising the small things of life as if gathering in a clutch of slippery fish.

*

Once she is over the worst, Elisabeth returns to Little Oaks. Life here has shifted from an energetic attempt at self-sufficiency to routine drudgery. Elisabeth's enthusiasm for sharing the house and for making do has reached its limit. She writes that, 'despite having successfully lowered my standard of living to a certain extent as befits war conditions there are some things I feel I shall <u>never</u> learn to stand – dirty butter dishes, stained table cloths, beer bottles standing about everywhere, washing hanging up in the kitchen at breakfast time, poultry making messes on the verandah. Robert's dining room manners, the smell and smoke of frying <u>right</u> through the house & so on & so on.' Sometimes Elisabeth has to escape the house, with its errant rabbits, disorder and broken plumbing, and goes to stay with friends. These trips give her a chance to recuperate and seem like 'Quite pre-war days, with eggs & sausages for breakfast, & chicken for lunch.' Once again, she finds a way to manage the difficult times by punctuating them with some respite and a shift in focus.

The book of lists is a mirror which reflects these fluctuations in Elisabeth's life and in her identity – from a hopeful young diplomatic wife to a determinedly hardworking wartime mother, and then out the other side, back to a life overseas as the shadows of war recede. I can map her movements through these years in the pages of objects and belongings, in the waves of diary entries, as I can map her journeys across the globe.

Again and again, the diaries and lists collide and I feel elated: Elisabeth describes the hot water system being broken and having to lug pails of water upstairs for the children's baths, and in her list book I find a scrawled note about plumbing where she obviously grabbed the closest thing to hand to write down instructions. Another diary entry notes: 'The hens have laid 37 eggs this week. We are now contemplating hatching out a clutch of duck's eggs – quite an amusing idea.' When I find a matching tally in her Egg Register, her diary breathes life into the list.

*

I want to visit Parham, the house in Sussex that offered Elisabeth solace during her depressions, and I arrange with the owner to have a tour. It is open to the public now, and it is odd thinking of all these people traipsing along the corridors of a place that was so special to Elisabeth. I drive through the large stone gateway and along a road lined with fields either side. I note the place where a German plane was shot down, as Elisabeth described, the old landmarks replaced suddenly by debris and destruction.

The house is Elizabethan, its gentle grey walls draped in wisteria. There is a fountain outside the entrance, and I remember reading Elisabeth's accounts of people jumping in it at parties. Inside the house, I can see why Elisabeth found such comfort here – there is an air of stillness and quiet beauty as well as the usual stately home furnishings and portraits of my ancestors. I think of my own slightly shabby, modest house and, not for the first time, have a sense of how different my life is from Elisabeth's, just two generations away. I touch the velvet back of a chair and imagine Elisabeth sitting in it, drawing closer to the fire, nursing a mug of hot cocoa and trying to piece together her scattered mind. And she is there, suddenly, in a photograph on one of the display boards, selling flags in Wandsworth to raise money for a hospital.

She had a hangover, I recall from her diary, and after only three hours sleep was not feeling as benevolent as she appears in the picture. It is strange seeing this picture on the wall at Parham, and I find it again, later, in one of Elisabeth's albums. It reminds me that she exists for other people and in their

Elisabeth selling flags

history, as much as she does in mine. Yet I feel covetous of her – territorial, even – as if they can't know what I know.

An archivist takes me down to a basement office where the family papers are stored. There are more photographs of Elisabeth and we talk about her time there, how the house rescued her. The archivist says, softly, 'She was not a well woman,' and I feel momentarily winded. I wonder what she means, struck by the fact that no one has described Elisabeth like this to me before – usually people recall her sense of humour or kindness, but it becomes clear that she was also defined in part by her illnesses. Perhaps the confident, capable front that she tried to portray slipped more than she knew. There is a vulnerability in her that lived alongside her vivaciousness and the confidence she exuded as a diplomat's wife, and it did not go unobserved.

I wonder who she was to those who knew her best. My uncle Samuel wrote a brief description of her: 'good at tennis & dancing, kind & protective, generous, liked Guinness, tried to stop smoking on an electric cigarette but people were always trying to light it, liked Am Dram, no proper home'. For her children (and her friends), she was so much more than someone they lost, more than someone who had spells of not being well – she was loving, funny, captivating, charming. Hers was an extraordinary life, despite its sadnesses. I walk around the grounds, finding a stunning walled garden in which I imagine Elisabeth and the evacuees picking fruit for their jam-making. I breathe in the air and the sun. Elisabeth feels so alive to me at this moment that I wish my mother were here to feel it too.

8

Beirut

BEIRUT.

Clothes Est. wholesale _ _ _ _ For actual expenditure, see further.

Geeny: Suit £25   Me: v Linen coat + skirt   18 gns.
       Socks   3   v Flowered afternoon dress
       Shoes   4   (made up, Fr. silk)   13 gns.
       Undies   5   Chinese satin, made up. 5 gns.
            £37 → Say £40   v Flowered chiffon, make up 7 gns.
S. & C. 3 winter vests each v 1 less smart A-dress   4 gns.
        3 "   pants "   v 2 more cottons   4 gns.
S. & C. Bibs for C.   v   Hats? Yellow Black straw
   4 prs. shoes. £3   v   gloves   3 gns.
   Summer coats. £10   Staff v Stockings   3 gns.
   2 "   suits   " v   2 good Blouses   6 gns.
   Material   £5   v   Slacks   2 gns.
 { Jumpers   £4   Shalls   1 gn.
 { wool   Sports shirts, 2.   4 gn.
   Socks   £1   2 Jumpers   3 gns.
   C's winter coat? £2   2 good wool dresses 20 gns.
            £25   Shoes, 2 prs.   4 gns.
                                      Approx. £90. ?

Car   £100   Undies   10
Linen £20   £   100.
Glass + China ?

IN 1944, AFTER TWO YEARS AT LITTLE OAKS, THE FAMILY is posted overseas: to Beirut. Gerry flies ahead in August, and Elisabeth and the children stay behind until they can join him. They leave the house that has witnessed their hopes for self-sufficiency, Elisabeth's small triumphs at domesticity, her awful second bout of postnatal depression, and the pressures of two families cohabiting in wartime conditions. Their belongings, duly listed and organised by Elisabeth, are packed into a van, including the hens and henhouse (which has been strapped to the back), with Gerry sitting on a chair in amongst all the furniture.

More lists, more packing, but this time Elisabeth has two small children and Nanny (who is now working for Elisabeth) in tow. The lead-up to the journey to Beirut is a difficult one: the Foreign Office has given them hardly any notice and there are complications getting out of the lease on Little Oaks. Elisabeth, Nanny and the children stay in a hotel in Surrey, but there are long delays finalising arrangements and Elisabeth is forced to take a short lease on a flat in Sevenoaks until plans for their journey are settled. At the end of December the family finally set off on a troopship to Egypt, from where they will travel overland to Beirut.

This is Elisabeth's sixth move since her marriage and I find myself feeling sorry for her, making all these lists and enduring difficult journeys to another unfamiliar place. But life at Little Oaks had become oppressive. Perhaps she will be happier in another country, better able to keep her inner world steady when her outer world is exotic and new.

*

Just as Elisabeth is embarking on another overseas adventure, I hit a low point. I am feeling utterly stuck and unsure in my life and doubting my ability to tell Elisabeth's story, when a package arrives in the post. It is a small jiffy bag, sent by my mother, who doesn't yet exist when Elisabeth sets off for Beirut and whom I am impatient to meet in this parallel world I have entered. It reminds me of another envelope that arrived recently, after we had all been to visit my mother and stepfather. We had left behind one playing card and a small sock. My mother had packaged these up and sent them on with a short note, in case we needed them. I was struck by the realisation that soon there would be no more of these little parcels of objects we have left behind.

Inside this jiffy bag is a book containing such heartbreak and hope that I have to sit down before I read it. The cover is tatty and the bottom of the pages have become scuffed and shredded. On the inside front cover, Gerry has written: 'During Elisabeth's final illness it was suggested that she should try to distract herself by writing a novel. Alas, she

was fading fast when she began it, and after a day or two had
no more strength to continue it. The beginning is of course
drawn from her passage to Beirut on a troopship.' And here
it is, across seven pages, the next part of Elisabeth's story,
written in her own words. It is as though she is the force
behind this book I am writing. She is here at my shoulder.

*

None of her pre-war passengers would have recognised the
ship in her present role. Gone are her days of leisurely luxury
cruises, her beautiful gleaming paintwork now obliterated
to comply with the current regulations regarding camou-
flage; her saloons and lounges are bare of their thick springy
carpets, the deep chairs and sparkling glass-topped coffee
tables. She slips through a grey and dreary Mediterranean,
one of a convoy of ships bound for Suez and on through the
canal to Bombay. It is dusk and there are no visible lights
on deck, not even the amber glow of a cigarette. A military-
police sentry shifts the weight from one foot to another and
nods to a passing passenger, checking they have the requisite
lifebelt with them.

Elisabeth, her two young boys and Nanny are part of a
small civilian contingent who have waited for weeks to
get a place on the ship. They are heading to Beirut, to join
Gerry and set up home in an apartment Elisabeth has seen
only hastily scribbled sketches of, folded inside letters full of
anxious questions about whether it is acceptable to have a
bathroom on the ground floor and worries that she will not
like the place Gerry has chosen. The other civilian passengers

include a judge travelling to Jerusalem to deal with a number of unusually awkward cases in the Palestinian courts, a colonial governor returning to his post in India, and an admiral who contrives to remain strictly incognito whilst devising important military strategies in his head. It is an uncomfortable voyage, with passengers crammed four or five to a cabin intended for one, and sitting down to meals like schoolchildren on long wooden benches at a bare table. The lounge has a few chairs but not enough to go around, so people sit on the floor, talking in low voices about the war.

The children are hungry. Nanny bustles briskly around the tiny cabin. 'You're surely not going along to supper in those awful old things,' she tuts as she looks disapprovingly at Elisabeth's slacks. 'Just been along to see if I could get the steward to give me a drop of hot water to rinse out your stockings, darling. Stupid idle lot those stewards are! Can't think what they're meant to *be*, I'm sure. All they do is stand around and pinch those giggling A.T.S. girls as they go by.'

Nanny sits down, takes off her shoes and gives her corns an encouraging rub before continuing: 'I wonder how we'll manage for laundries and such, Beirut doesn't sound too civilized to me, dear.'

Samuel is peering out of the window, trying to spot the crisp white of a navy uniform. Elisabeth scoops up her younger son, who toppled forwards with a muffled yelp as the ship lurched suddenly. She smiles and replies, 'I'll tell you exactly how we'll manage for laundries. There'll be an old woman who'll come and squat in the back yard beside a large bowl filled from the garden pump, and she'll scrub and rinse the linen and sing in a high-pitched voice – and probably drive you mad because you don't think she's doing it thoroughly.' Nanny looks sternly over the rims of her round spectacles, and then her face softens. She has accompanied Elisabeth overseas many times, and buries her excitement beneath a tight-bunned scepticism.

'Time for supper,' she replies. 'You have to be devilish punctual if you don't want your tepid tomato soup to be stone cold.' They bundle the children, and all four lifebelts, out onto the deck. The air is sharp with salt and sea winds. They sail on, towards another new life.

*

In the words of Jorge Luis Borges, 'I do not know which of us has written this page.' Most of the preceding words are Elisabeth's. With her words, as with her lists, she has carried us on to another place, another time. So, here we are: Beirut, 1 January 1945.

When Elisabeth, Nanny and the children arrive in Cairo, they have to wait for three days in a bug-ridden hotel whilst it rains continuously outside (and inside: the roof leaks). They then travel by train for sixteen hours to Haifa, where Gerry meets them and brings them to their new apartment in the city.

Lebanon is an exciting, unstable, vibrant place. It feels familiar to Elisabeth, reminding her of the time she spent in Persia in her youth, and she loves the sparse Middle Eastern terrain. She used to enjoy painting watercolours of land-scapes, and seemed to be acutely attuned to the push and pull of nature's rhythms. As a young woman she was moved by the way these places affect her senses of smell and touch. She loved sitting in the 'pomegranate garden', sketching and writing, and her diary contains an enchanted description of a picnic in 'Death Valley': 'It was quiet and shady, and smelt of wild mignonette…It was fantastic and unreal. Beetles the size of a thumb swam solemnly up and down, birds perched on slender trees that bend beneath their weight, a dead crab lay on the bank. And over it brooded the hills. A…voller [?] flashed past us like a streak of blue summer-lightning. I felt I was dreaming. Somehow it was all too like a fairy-story to be true. And yet it was beautiful and the feeling of remoteness it inspired was pleasant and lingered for hours…'

The new posting to Lebanon reawakens Elisabeth's love for this bare, ancient continent with its landskeins of stony hills, sandy folds of desert and mountainous borders. Edgar Allan Poe wrote of these desert places:

> Among the rabble – men,
> Lion ambition is chain'd down…
> Not so in deserts where the grand
> The wild – the terrible conspire…

There is something in this beautiful, dreadful expansiveness that draws Elisabeth in. Lebanon itself is small and runs in flanks from north to south, first the lush Mediterranean coast, then the steep mountains of the Mount Lebanon range, on to the semi-desert of the northern Bekaa valley and its more fertile southern area, and up to the mountains on the border with Syria.

Like the landscape, the people of Lebanon are distinct yet interconnected: the majority are Shiite Muslims but there are large populations of Sunnis, Druze and Maronite Christians. In 1945 the British are wrestling with the problems resulting from attacks by both Jews and Arabs unhappy with how Palestine, under British mandate, is being ruled. The government is concerned about securing British post-war national interests in the turbulent Middle East. French colonial rule in Lebanon ended in 1943 and Gerry and Elisabeth arrive as it moves towards independence under the watch of Allied troops. Violence, or the threat of it, is never far away.

At the end of a two-page list of china that is being transported or stored, Elisabeth sketches the layout of their new home so that she can work out where to put things, and how they will fit into the space in this bustling city. She is relieved to be 'in a blaze of light again, & surrounded by fruit, beauty parlours, chocolate shops etc'. The apartment Gerry has found them is surrounded by a jumble of Ottoman-era and colonial-style buildings, and stone red-roofed houses. Traffic policemen stand in the middle of the wide streets under umbrellas, while the souks, with their piles of produce laid out on the ground and sellers carrying baskets on their backs, provide a cluttered contrast to the palm-lined avenues. Small beaches dot the bay and people swim from jetties in the still blue sea. The land beyond the city rears up to mountainous peaks, some of them laced with snow. These mountains envelop the city, making the baking heat in summer almost unbearable, and many families escape to the villages in the hills during these months.

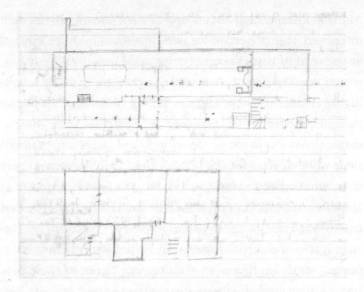

Elisabeth's sketch of the flat in Beirut

The hillsides beyond Beirut are spattered with olive groves and citrus orchards, and carpeted with wild poppies and cranesbill. Abandoned terraces cut into the slopes are now used for grazing, circled from above by buzzards and harriers. Armoured-car convoys occasionally snake along the dirt roads, passing through desert valleys populated by larks and jackal. Ruins of medieval crusader castles or ancient cities rise up out of the landscape, home now to fruit bats and swifts. It is harsh terrain, but there is a purity and poetry woven into it. This is the place that Elisabeth will call home for the next two years, where she will unpack and raise her two small boys and once more step into the role of embassy wife.

*

Many of Elisabeth's lists concern clothes – items to be bought or packed, things needed for herself or the children. The list at the start of this chapter sets out all the clothes the family would need in Beirut. It is one of her most vivid lists, conjuring images of these clothes, neatly folded and packed. I imagine the feel of the wispy fabric of the flowered chiffon dress, the smoothness of the gloves, and the softness of the little woollen vests for the boys. Sometimes clothes are more than what someone wears; they actually seem to be part of them. I once owned a dark-grey pin-striped jacket that had belonged to my paternal grandfather, who died when I was two. It had been kept, unworn, by my father in various cupboards, until I decided it was the perfect accoutrement to my 1980s ensemble. I loved the weight of the fabric and the fact that it had little bits of tobacco stuck in the seams of the pockets (my grandfather was a heavy smoker, a habit which precipitated his premature death). I would pick at these tiny leaves and imagine his form inside the jacket. I recall putting on that exquisite, long-lost Dior dress of Elisabeth's, the dress that now lies, fragile as a cobweb, in my attic. The fabric is like a leaf's skeleton, thin and easily torn.

The suits, evening coats and dresses noted in Elisabeth's clothes lists demonstrate the informal 'uniform' diplomats' wives were required to wear. They needed to appear elegant, sophisticated, in control, approachable yet of a certain status. It brings with it an expectation of conformity to the social mores or rules of the organisation, an inevitable subjugation of the individual to the group she represents.

Elisabeth had a keen eye for a well-made dress and took an

interest in couture, but also in what everyday people – particularly the Lebanese people around her – were wearing. In 1940s Lebanon clothes were quite traditional, and the different religious concessions were recognisable by their attire. The Druze and Bedouin men wore distinctive types of jackets and Shi'a women wore long dresses, but there were also similarities across these groups, with men wearing *labbade*, baggy trousers, and women predominantly wearing a veil. During Elisabeth's time there, the obligation to wear the veil was being questioned as part of a growing women's movement in the region, which had long campaigned for reform of education, marital law and the legal status of women, as well as national self-determination. Now, alongside the movement for political independence from the colonial powers, the women's rights movement was gathering momentum. As an independent-minded foreign woman, forging her own way as a wife in the rigidly patriarchal diplomatic community, Elisabeth watches these matters of women's social status and influence closely. In a diary entry from 1936 she noted that diplomats were dependent on their women-folk: 'Mr Blackburn can do no work at all unless Mrs B. is around. Ha! The influence of women, tra-la, tra-la.'

For Gerry, diplomatic occasions often required an actual uniform. The photographs of Foreign Office uniforms I find from the time are faux-militaristic, all plumes and brass buttons and swords, pomp and swagger, intended to convey a sense of authority and tradition. Gerry took an interest in clothes, and was of a generation whose parents exercised far more control over their offsprings' wardrobe than we parents do today – he writes of his father kitting him out for a trip to Austria in leather breeches so tight he couldn't bend his legs. He also claimed he had no calves, and I imagine Elisabeth having to reassure him that he looked acceptable all trussed up in his feathers and pomp, despite his odd-shaped legs. In later life, after he had put on weight, she sometimes had to sew him into his uniform trousers. There's something poignant about the fact that clothes remain essentially the same, while we change.

In the list overleaf, Elisabeth notes down the clothes that Samuel has outgrown, storing them for Charles and any future children. Memories are intertwined in their threads and this makes them worth keeping, and listing. Samuel leaves his own mark on the page, perhaps wanting to copy his mother, vying with the book of lists for her attention. We meet him on the page, amidst his too-small summer vests and dungarees.

I find what may be one of Elisabeth's first ever lists, typed up by Norton when they were young and living at home. Norton has embellished what would otherwise have been a simple list with statements like 'As dictated by her, with interjections of fury,' and 'Hats, she said calmly.' It is a playful inventory, a glimpse into the relationship between Elisabeth and her brother, innocently foreshadowing the horrors Elisabeth would endure in making the list of Norton's things following his death.

Now that Elisabeth is an adult, performing a proper, if ill-defined, role as a diplomat's wife, I sense an ambivalence in her – and in Gerry too – towards their social duties,

<u>S's old clothes</u> : (small suit-case) {1 blue
{1 yellow 1
Woollies 1 white romper (6 months) 1 pink {1 brown, 1 blue trousers
(all wool) New brown romper, + 1 pr. brown trousers,
5 assorted 1st & 2nd size jumpers + 2 crawlers, all worn.
2 Hand knitted over-vests
3 Summer vests (2 1st size, rather torn) 2 crochet bodices.
2 blue pyjamas (6 months) 5 summer rompers (Noris) 1 sunbonnet
1 Thick, blue crawling knickers
2 Smocks, cotton, 6 months
<u>Larger Things</u> green + check Viyella suit, 1yr -18 months. 2 jumpers (shop)
1 pyjama top + 2 trousers. 2 thick cotta knickers. 1 blue cotta shorts
1 dark blue Dungarees. 2 prs. Clarks shoes (4 & 5)
Yellow + white Bucket suit. Summer pram-cover.
Summer coat (18 months) New Blue smock.
For S. next summer 3 prs. print shirts, 1 white linen hat. Sand shoes
Size 7. Two prs. new shoes (e) 2 prs. brown cotta shorts.
3 Dungarees (large sizes) Grey flannel shorts: 6 unworn
cotta shirts (Tunky) 3 chilprufe vests, sleeved (4) 2 Size 3, twins

(as dictated by her.)
(with interjectidns
of fury.)

T   Part I--That show.

Coats & coatees.

    I Red-&-green tweed coat,thick.

    2 Beige coat,thin.

    3 Purple school coat,thick,& hideous at that.

    4 Light beige cloth coat & skirt,thin.

    5 Purple blazer.

    6 Red-&-green wool coatee,so to speak.

    7 Beige wool coatee.

Hats,she said calmly.

    I Purple felt hat.

    2 Purple straw hat.

    3 & 4 Berets,purple,twain of them.

    4 Brown plaited straw.

    5 Straw,beige,tagel,lace brim,with.

    6 Green stitched felt.

    7 White tennis felt. That's all of hats.

Now we come to thick frocks,etc.

    I Beige tweed frock,thinnish.

    2 Green three-piece suitee.

    3 Red-&-green tweed skirt,nuthatch.

    4 Tweed skirt,various colours,for country waer.

    5 Green djibbah. No more frocks & things.

Jumpers now.

    I Red-&-green striped,yes.

    2 Plain light green,thin.   Also two white ones in which I

    ~~xxxxx~~ Beige with darker stripes,3,that was.   sweat.

    4 Darkish greenish thickish jumper.

Now we......Bouses.

    I Jap silk blousee,white.

    2 Three new winter djibbah blouses,& three oldsters.

    8 Four summer ones,various trimmings. no more blouses.

Thin frocks,etc.

    Yaller silk taffetta frockee.
      No I evening.no ill-feeling.

sometimes relishing the parties and glamour but at other times longing to be at home in the quiet of the countryside chopping wood or reading. In *Wolf Hall* Hilary Mantel describes Thomas Cromwell 'arranging his face', the gathering and setting of a particular expression designed to convey exactly what he intends to be seen. Getting dressed is like this: we are performing as a character and selecting the right costume. If we need confidence in a job interview, we reach for a sharp suit; if we are heading out for a night of dancing and merriment, we may try to portray youthful vim. We do not *discover* our identity, we *create* it, through the clothes we wear, the belongings with which we surround ourselves, our values, and our relationships with others. Identity is malleable, permeable and fluid, and the clothes we choose are one strand connecting our idea of the self to the outside world.

But clothes can also reveal much that we would rather remained hidden. I recall Norton's pink dressing gown and the coat in which he died, one an expression of a forbidden self and the other a shroud for the external self. The fabric with which we surround ourselves carries an imprint of who we are. This ghostly shadow-self can often be as illuminating as the polished, or dishevelled, self we project to the world.

Blake Morrison writes movingly about going through his dead father's wardrobe looking for things to keep, making a list of his own: 'his 1947 white cotton tennis shirt with his name-tag sewn in red on the collar; his bomber jacket, his velvet waistcoat, his flat golf cap…now that he's gone I feel like a grave robber. I take three jumpers, a dozen pairs of socks, two pairs of brown leather shoes, some old cufflinks…

Then I put on this white nylon shirt, black tie, grey suit, black woollen socks, black shoes. I am going to his funeral in his clothes.' Joan Didion also describes how she was able to be quite rational about disposing of her husband's possessions after he died, but she was not able to get rid of her husband's shoes, because she felt he would need them when he got back. In these circumstances, clothes keep people alive in our world; we imagine the form of their bodies filling out the fabric, animating each piece, we remember when they wore the garments, flashing back in time. Clothes can bring people back.

Elisabeth's accounts and lists of expenditure show large amounts spent on her bespoke dresses and suits, far more than seems necessary now. But the clothes were more to Elisabeth than just outfits. In one of her diaries, she wrote of her belief in the importance of cleanliness and a neat appearance, alongside mental stimulation, in keeping a person happy: 'I look upon cleanliness & as much beauty as possible to be of the utmost importance. One knows oneself how much pleasanter life is when surrounded by attractive, cared-for people. Thus a quick bath every day, well-brushed hair, clean neat nails etc etc are essential, as are clean clothes & pleasant unfidgeting habits – no useless fiddling or anything.' Clothes enabled Elisabeth to maintain her public persona as well as bolstering her self-esteem. She hopes that stepping into her uniform of flowered chiffon will help her make the transition from housewife and mother to diplomat's wife.

*

Elisabeth always struggles at the start of a posting, and Beirut is no different. She feels low and rarely writes in her diary – there is one mention of a picnic in the apricot orchards of a minister's country house in Damascus, but otherwise she busies herself with the children and organising social events for the embassy. Diplomatic parties are frequent and often not much fun: 'Some of the rich Lebanese parties are rather revolting: their marble palaces, hideously expensively-dressed women, sumptuous rich food, lace tablecloths & so on – it does seem such a contrast to England during the war, & presumably still more of a contrast to other miserable European countries.' She is uncomfortable with the overt display of wealth, and feels she doesn't fit in. She is even unsure about how to 'housekeep' here, writing that she wants to do a good job but that this involves devoting at least two hours per day to domestic chores, despite having three domestic servants. The children are scatty with excitement and dislocation; they need her time and energy to adjust to their new home.

After struggling to get by for the first three months in Beirut, she begins to feel better and settles into her new life: 'I've started to come to again with a sigh of relief, & started to enjoy life & not let the housekeeping get me down too much.' She notes details like picking the purple anemones and cyclamen on the way home from a day at the beach in February – a sign that her world is coming right again.

There is a background tension in diplomatic circles in Beirut, despite the relief brought by the end of the war. The British and French are clashing over French influence in the Levant and there are also small incidents, like a man being knocked out in the dark and a French woman hitting a British officer over the head with a bottle, where these tensions bubble over into ex-pat life. Elisabeth describes 'bowing politely to French generals attending the same functions', implying a mutual suspension of mistrust.

There are tensions within the Lebanese population, too. As the economy shifts from agriculture to commerce and trade, wealth becomes more polarised: the poverty of the peasant villages is a stark contrast to the slick cosmopolitan elite in Beirut. Add to this the influx of refugees fleeing the turmoil in neighbouring states and the ever-present religious divisions, and it is clear that the country is ripe for some kind of violent eruption. International problems between the French and the Syrians have damaged diplomatic relations between France and Britain, and the diplomats in Lebanon are charged with stabilising the region and minimising French influence.

Despite the importance of Gerry's mission, this is a sociable posting, and there are plenty of diplomatic events to attend, often in the gruelling heat. Elisabeth writes: 'Gerry & I really did our duty thoroughly, being the only members of the staff who bothered to represent the Legation at the various functions for the troops organised by the Lebanese government...We sweated away, attending gymkhanas, race-meetings, sports etc...'

As in Madrid, Elisabeth's diary becomes a place to record both the serious and the absurd: 'Gerry has had quite a few crises...first, with the Palestine situation as it is, we had our bombscare – with the attempt to blow up the Consulate and

Elisabeth at an embassy party

the American Legation. A few days later Mrs Wadsworth suddenly dropped dead…and the "quarter" adored the gossip it
caused. One of the communal typists was then killed coming
home from a dance on the back of a soldier's motorbicycle.
Mr F indulged in his usual intermittent drinking bouts &
G had to tell him he would shortly be sacked. The Shones
were appointed to India & returned here for a brief whirl of
exhausting farewell parties…Sophie [Shone] had a boil on
her bottom which she delighted in describing, and it kept her
from attending several of the parties.'

*

During the summer months in Lebanon, Elisabeth moves
the boys up into the Chouf mountains, to a village called
Chemlan. Not long after Gerry and Elisabeth leave Lebanon,

a so-called 'spy school' is set up by the British government in this very village, aimed at educating intelligence officers and infiltrating Arab society. But in Elisabeth's time it is a quiet place. The family's belongings are loaded into a Legation truck and transported to their summer home, which Elisabeth describes as: 'simple & gloriously easy to run – a big square living-room opening onto the verandah – five bedrooms & the kitchen all around…Even the catering seems easier: a man calls for orders of an evening, & eggs etc. are always easily obtainable. Drinking water is brought round daily in 2 big czuches.' She loves sitting on the verandah in the evenings, looking out over olive groves and the mountains sloping down to the sea beyond.

Life in Chemlan is not a holiday, however, and Gerry's work continues. There are frequent overnight guests and the usual diplomatic emergencies to contend with. Elisabeth describes one hectic evening when Gerry was heavily embroiled in a telephone conversation, lying on the floor talking to the Prime Minister while a supper guest took shorthand dictation. The lights fused and everyone rushed to find candles, meanwhile space had to be found for an additional guest, so young Charles, asleep in his cot, was moved into another room. Later that evening, Elisabeth had to try to find a car to take Gerry back into Beirut.

The family also socialise with their local neighbours, although this is not always a success: 'The ensuing meal was a nightmare of stuffed intestines, yards of them, & things like rats turned inside out & filled with grey-coloured rice. Each time I left a particularly revolting bit on one side my

Cocktail Protégé . Feb. 16

80 people invited . . . . .

—

Sandwiches — 3 loaves of bread 1.10. pkts . margarine (L.5.50)
3 Tins Sardines   1.50.
12 Eggs & tomato 4.
4 gm Olives   60 Cheese puffs . L.15.
Cream cheese & olive   Walnuts   3.86
Spam .   (Abt. 350 - 400 Sandwiches in all)
                    Tips . L.35
1 Cold Cooked Turkey (L.40)   Accordn. L.30
2 Tins Spam   L.1.20.
½ Kilo Ham   L. 9.
40 Crab Patties (2 Tins crawfish) L.3.
2 Large mousses of Tongue L.12.
1 bowl Russian salad , 1 bowl Cabbage salad. L.8.
2 Large bowls ice-cream (136) + 60 biscuits (L.7)
60 Bread Rolls (Nafi.) 2

Drink : Tomato juice (2 Tins) Grapefruit & gin   Cup (4 white wine
. . . Martinis   Whisky   + 2 soda water
                                              + 1 brandy)

host pounced on me & said I was missing the best part!' A happier meal was a feast in the Bekaa Valley; Elisabeth rode in a procession of twenty vehicles, surrounded by Arab horsemen firing rifles and jostling the car, and ate delicious food.

Back in Beirut after the summer, she turns to her list book once again, planning and recording the food for various parties she must throw, feeding an endless stream of guests and dignitaries. This list encapsulates Elisabeth's role as a diplomatic wife.

It is one of many similar lists in Elisabeth's book, which reveal a smorgasbord of culinary offerings: bread rolls, salmon salad, kidney and sausage pilau, raspberry fool, passion-fruit cream, a chestnut pyramid, lemon tart, cheese straws, fruit salad, stuffed eggs, sardine balls, biscuits and cheese, dates, olives, nuts, jellies, asparagus patties, shrimp patties, cakes, sandwiches, spaghetti and meatballs, tongue mousse, potato salad, jam tarts, melons, meat roll, ham, chicken, Russian salad. Diplomats' wives were obviously constrained by the food available wherever they were posted, and many additional supplies had to be shipped in from London. The requirement to put on a lavish spread, regardless of the political and economic circumstances in which they were living, meant women running diplomatic households were under significant pressure. In the face of food shortages, as Elisabeth experienced in Madrid, wives and cooks often had to find inventive ways to stretch resources and flavours.

The food in this list suggests a civilised but not overly showy party with a strongly British feel – there are few local dishes, possibly because embassies were expected to provide guests with a taste of food from their home country. I try to imagine what the ingredients in this and other lists would become. Olives were perhaps to be rolled in the Petit Suisse cheese and then wrapped in the ham, lobster to be made into croquettes, and peaches pressed into pastry cases and baked in the tartlet moulds Elisabeth notes she must buy. She orders around 350 sandwiches, to be made by the embassy staff. There would be drink, lots of it, and dancing. Connections would be made and political discussions veiled in the shimmery gauze and quivering smoke of a cocktail party.

As well as listing the food she provided, Elisabeth also kept records of the drinks required for all this entertaining: sherry, gin, vermouth, whisky and soda, Kia-Ora, grapefruit and gin, tomato juice, cider cup, pineapple cocktail, barrels of beer. I think again, reading this, how difficult it must have been for Gerry to moderate his drinking when it was so bound up with his job and who he was supposed to be. Entertaining took up a considerable part of the household budget – Elisabeth kept detailed accounts of their monthly expenditure, which reveal that most months the largest sum was spent on food. Alongside the food listed above, there is a scribbled pencil calculation, possibly totting up how much the canapés and cocktails would cost. I study Elisabeth's lists and discover that in one month she had to cater for fifty-six people for tea, twenty for cocktails and twenty-seven to lunch and dinner; another month she had thirteen people to tea, a hundred to cocktails and sixty-three to lunch and dinner. Heads and plates must have been spinning.

When they weren't catering for guests, Elisabeth and

Gerry also ate the local cuisine: salty flatbreads, hummus, tahini, baba ghanouge, tabbouleh, beans, sweetmeats, salted yoghurt, preserves and pickles, strong Arabic coffee flavoured with cardamom, orange-blossom tea, arak and *jallab* (a drink made from dates, grape molasses and rose water, served with ice, pine nuts and raisins). These colourful, flavoursome dishes are still staples of Lebanese home cooking and reflect the landscape – the citrus groves and crops of the fertile southern Bekaa Valley. The contrast with the bland, austere meals Elisabeth had to prepare under rationing just a few months ago must have been stark, and I wonder whether these new tastes wove their way into Elisabeth's ordinary cooking.

I think of my mother's approach to cooking and look for some echo of her travels in the meals she prepared for us as children. But she doesn't really enjoy cooking and chooses dishes that don't have too many 'stages'. We were raised on home-cooked but pretty standard 1970s and 1980s fare: Angel Delight, shepherd's pie, and our favourite dish, penne pasta. She did believe, however, that we should always have a pudding and, despite being a single mother for much of the time we were growing up, she always prepared something sweet to finish with.

*

As a child, I imagined Gerry and Elisabeth existing in a permanent state of pearl-dripping, cocktail-swilling giddiness, cigarettes jauntily waving from elegant holders as dancers swept around the floor. There are moments in Elisabeth's letters and diaries that zing with the excitement of this strange peripatetic existence. The landscapes, people and constantly shifting cultures mean that life is never boring, and Elisabeth thrives on the buzz. But her lists reveal the enormous effort it took to manage her world. As in Peking and Madrid, she becomes exhausted, unable to find a balance between monotonous domesticity and the fast pace of diplomatic life. A letter Gerry wrote to his mother in 1940, from their posting in Madrid, reveals what a strain Elisabeth sometimes finds things: 'Poor E is wretched. I never see her except at meals or in bed; and the meals are always parties, and by bed-time – 2.30 a.m. usually – we are both too tired to make sense.' He was often bored and frustrated in his work, wanting to sink his teeth into some juicy international negotiations or pummel some important hands instead of attending tedious parties. Perhaps this fuelled his drinking. I recall a snippet from a letter Gerry wrote to his parents years before, when he was just starting out in diplomatic life, which encapsulates the bizarre nature of this work: 'If you could…let me have a dozen <u>good</u> tennis balls, my chance of finding out how things are here would be much improved.'

Sometimes Elisabeth needs to escape the confines of embassy life. In 1946, she goes on an excursion, with three male friends, to Petra, the 2,000-year-old Jordanian city carved into the rose-gold rock. To get there, Elisabeth embarks on a complicated journey by car, driving along roads lined on one side with olive groves and red-topped houses, and on the other by the Mediterranean lapping at the beach. The party stay in a bedbug-festooned hotel and then travel by trolley bus across Amman and on by car up the desert plain, through parched, desiccated countryside. She sees grey foxes, desert owls, speeding gazelle, herds of camel and black Bedouin tents. She rides in a taxi so dilapidated that the seat is bare horsehair, and so cramped that she has to sit with her legs twined round the gearstick and brake. It is dusty and hot and she loves it.

The final leg of the journey is on horseback, riding on double-pommelled Arabian saddles down steep gorges, surrounded by clattering mule boys. A boy carries their lunch on his head, running alongside them, the sandwiches bouncing up and down as he runs (which results in ruination as the food becomes 'one anonymous mass...all mashed up... bananas, hard-boiled eggs, baked potatoes'). The ancient city reveals itself at the end of a deep, dark gorge spotted with oleander flowers, black rocks rising on each side and only a narrow band of blue sky above. Elisabeth is awestruck by the setting, and by the tombs, Treasury, banquet halls and baths carved into the imposing sandstone. It is a welcome wilderness and provides a respite from her diplomatic duties.

Aside from the rigmarole of keeping to the Foreign Office's rules, sometimes the people are just as hard to endure. Elisabeth and Gerry try to be delightful and amusing, but even their good-natured hospitality is occasionally stretched, as revealed in this letter from Gerry (written from Paris in 1957) to Elisabeth: 'I was having a bath to remove my agricultural sweat before going to the Colombian National Day...I was button-holed by that frightful little man Frangelis of the Acad. Int. de Droit, who spat egg sandwich all over me while gripping me firmly by the arm and explaining about Aranco and the Sultan of Oman.'

Elisabeth also describes how, towards the end of their posting in Beirut, she pays a visit to a wealthy acquaintance, whom she finds wearing a turban and reclining on a divan at the end of a long hall hung with carpet and brocade. The woman complains of being exhausted by all the charity work she is doing. Her latest cause is a fundraising ball for poor people who used to be rich, and she bemoans the huge amount of effort she is putting into caring for a pig that is to be raffled at the ball. She drawls, 'I have to feed it with bottles of milk every few hours. You <u>can't</u> trust these maids! They might even sell the milk & give it WATER! Then I <u>can't</u> decide what its dress should be made of, and I've got the cradle to decorate. Ah, I am *extrêmement fatiguée* with all this work!' Elisabeth's own trials and tribulations organising cocktail parties might seem equally laughable to other, less fortunate women of her time (and our own), but I can't help smiling at her comical pen portrait of this woman and her well-coddled pig.

*

In the 1940s, when Elisabeth is a fledgling diplomatic wife, the British Foreign Office is becoming less elitist (most diplomats traditionally followed a well-worn path from public school via Oxbridge), but the role of women is still ambiguous. Women are unpaid and there is no formal structure or defined job, yet they are seen as vital to creating the right atmosphere and conditions for the formal work of the diplomats. It is as if a wife is a 'two-for-the-price-of-one' bonus, the work they do acknowledged but not officially recognised. They are judged alongside their husbands but receive no substantive appraisal for their work, and often feel under significant pressure to maintain standards in very difficult circumstances.

Later, from 1946, women are able to become career diplomats, but they face great prejudice and assumptions about their abilities. Unmarried women in an embassy are regarded as potentially liable to cause sex scandals and are subjected to unpleasant speculation about their moral standing. It is interesting that in Elisabeth's unfinished novel her main character is a woman who has just been made the first female ambassador. Clearly, Elisabeth holds strong views on the position of women within the diplomatic service and believes they should receive due recognition for the work they do. Perhaps she entertained ambitions to do something similar herself.

Women are always on duty – the notion of being 'in service' is deeply entrenched – and they have to uphold strict rules of etiquette, like remaining at a party until the last guest has left, and waiting on the pavement for the ambassador's car to drive off before they can move. Houses are not private sanctuaries but are considered part of the embassy, and hosting parties is seen as the primary public duty of a wife, as well as putting up visitors, often at short notice and for unspecified lengths of time. Wives also often perform a secretarial role, and Elisabeth is skilled at deciphering and encoding, helping out when Gerry has too much work or if there is a crisis. She sometimes writes in her diaries and list book in Chinese to avoid sensitive information being discovered. Even these private things are not completely hers.

Many women are posted to countries that feel alien and unthinkably remote from their normal lives. Some have an isolated existence, especially if their embassy is in a compound, constrained by cultural values and their duties, dependent on the people within the embassy for friendship and guidance. Within the embassy, life for women is just as hierarchical as it is for their husbands, with the ambassador's wife at the top and the rest of the women supporting her. Elisabeth's life is influenced by the women to whom she has to defer, as she describes in this outpouring of frustration with one ambassadress: '[She] is in bed with a bronchial cold – which does not prevent her, however, from fussing unceasingly on the telephone, & making life hideous for the embassy wives. Never in my life have I met anyone with such a capacity for inventing totally unnecessary jobs for other people. How I loathe her.'

But ambassadors can be amusingly eccentric, as well as difficult to work with. Cynthia Gladwyn, an ambassadress in Paris, writes of one previous ambassador who frequently took to bed or simply disappeared when faced with stressful political or international situations, and whose wife 'had embarked on a history of the world beginning in the year 2000 BC, [and] ingeniously planned to inform the reader what was going on in all parts of the globe at the same time. To write this ambitious work she would retire up a tree in the garden from where, when she was needed, a footman fetched her by whistling below.' For a strong-minded and intelligent woman like Elisabeth, it is sometimes a trial to have to maintain a neutral, statesmanlike façade when working with unpredictable or incompetent embassy superiors and their dotty wives.

There can be gossip and sniping too among the diplomatic wives. Elisabeth's mother was once criticised for her impersonal style of entertaining. She was actually painfully shy and found the public aspect of her role extremely difficult, so the jibe must have further undermined her confidence.

Servants and domestic help can make a great difference to the life of a lonely diplomatic wife, and are more important on an overseas posting than at home. Gerry writes amusingly of some new servants who did not seem promising: 'The new couple are pretty frightful. He is an enormous trembling, wheezing Latvian oaf; she a little shawlie with a sharp eye, whose culinary motto seems to be "When in doubt, play the nutmeg". Mashed potatoes can be rendered surprisingly unpalatable in this simple manner. I think they are poisoning the coffee, but it may only be more nutmeg.' In the wake of the scandal in which Elisabeth's father's valet was exposed as a spy, Elisabeth must have been even keener to surround herself with loyal, dependable staff. In Nanny, she found a steady hand, a sensible adviser and precious friend. Elisabeth was kind, warm and friendly, a person whom other women trusted and on whom they depended, yet she writes of the other diplomatic wives with a mixture of amused fondness and disdain – she didn't develop any great or enduring friendships while living overseas. So far from home, letters become vital connections with real friends and family. The weekly 'bag' is eagerly anticipated, and any delays or lost mail feel disastrous.

Part of the women's sense of loneliness and isolation comes from being separated from their children. Younger children accompany their parents on postings, but the Foreign Office pays for staff to send their older children to boarding school in England, and there are regular and painful goodbyes. Worries for their children's safety, the possibility of diseases, the slowness of the journeys and vastness of the distances all challenge a mother's organisational skills and emotional reserves.

I imagine the feelings of relief, anticipation and shyness that children must have felt when they were reunited with their parents after long periods away, and the schisms created within a family's foundations. I recall some lines by W. S. Merwin: 'Your absence has gone through me / Like a thread through a needle. / Everything I do is stitched with its colour.' Although Samuel and Charles were too young to be sent back to England from Beirut, Elisabeth, Norton and Alethea would have experienced this shock of separation many times. Each rupture goes deeper, testing their mettle, until perhaps they don't feel anything any more. Left in the care of schoolteachers or relatives – as many boarding-school children are – they must ultimately rely on themselves. The journalist and author Deborah Blum writes, 'We grow best in soil cultivated by someone who thinks we matter;' all a separated parent can hope for is that the people to whom they have entrusted their children will think they matter.

In 1944, before leaving for Beirut, Elisabeth was reunited with her sister after nearly five years. They had written regularly over that time and sent patterns for dresses and parcels of fabric between England and Turkey. But in those five years their brother had killed himself and the sisters had not been able to console or comfort each other, and Elisabeth had had two children. The pressure on embassy wives to put their husband's position above all else, even family, is evident in the fact that Elisabeth's mother did not return home for Norton's funeral, or for the birth of Elisabeth's first child. I remember my mother flying across the world to meet my firstborn, arriving at our house in Melbourne, Australia, when he was two weeks old. It seemed as if they had known each other since the beginning of time. She put him over her shoulder and sang him a lullaby that Elisabeth had sung to her, and nothing felt more right than that moment. I feel sorry for Elisabeth that she couldn't witness this between her own babies and her mother, and sorry that she didn't get to be a grandmother herself.

*

Despite the challenges, Elisabeth mostly loves the diplomatic life. She enjoys being part of the action, being at the centre of the policy-making and treaty-wrangling that characterises the post-war settlement. She finds a way to channel her intelligence and wit into entertaining others, and being highly organised about her life. In her list book, we see an outlet for this desire to control a world that is mostly uncontrollable, where her belongings might need to be packed and accounted for at a moment's notice, where she may be required to conjure up hundreds of sandwiches and a jolly evening or nurse an ailing colleague when all she wants to do is go to bed. Her lists are almost works of art, existing as simple, pared-down expressions of her spirit.

Many diplomats' wives enjoyed being pioneers, travelling to places their contemporaries would never see, witnessing life abroad at close quarters. I think of Elisabeth's contemporary, the adventurer and intelligence-gatherer Freya Stark, travelling alone around the Middle East in the 1930s, driving an unreliable car across hundreds of miles of blazing desert. There are women doing extraordinary things in an apparently hostile landscape and amidst political turmoil.

Author Katie Hickman describes Countess Granville, wife of the ambassador to Paris in 1824: 'Here was a woman – intelligent, educated and of an independent disposition – with an urgent need to retain a sense of herself, and to create her own space, amidst the all-consuming but artificial trappings of her role.' This is how I see Elisabeth, finding a way to turn the work and mundanity of diplomatic life into a meaningful job. Her world was transitory, impermanent, highly charged; her lists are her counterweight, providing order and structure, and a record of the good work she has done.

*

November 1946. There are rumours that Gerry will be moved to a new posting and he eventually learns that the family is to be sent to Rio de Janeiro. They are pleased – South America is unfamiliar to them and will be an adventure. The two children, now aged five and three, are sent ahead in December with Nanny on a cargo boat loaded with oranges, to stay with Elisabeth's parents in Brussels while Gerry awaits orders. And so the stressful job of wrapping up a post begins: 'Our house is a sea of paper shavings & yawning packing cases,'

writes Elisabeth. The colleague who is due to replace Gerry
has come down with jaundice, and Elisabeth nurses him for
two weeks, impatient to leave and frustrated at the time it is
taking. Her boys are far, far away and she doesn't know when
she will see them. She organises farewell parties and Christmas parties, and then Gerry becomes unwell. In addition to
the organisational chaos, Elisabeth is knocked down in the
souk by a thief who is being pursued by a policeman. She
picks herself up, 'rather embarrassed as I had on somewhat
flimsy underwear. When I asked Mrs Joly [a bystander] if I'd
exposed myself indecently her answer was not reassuring: "It
was not for long," she said.'

Finally, on 19 January the luggage is packed, the lists ticked
off and Elisabeth and Gerry drive down to Haifa: 'It is a strain
getting away from a post! Gerry heaved sigh after sigh of relief
as we drove along the coast, & relapsed into torpor, only
murmuring now and then in his sleep.' There has just been a
Zionist bomb attack on the police headquarters in Haifa, and
they drive on to Jerusalem along a road that is deemed to have
had fewer explosions. Passing rumbling patrols of armoured
cars, they reach the port only to discover their boat will be
delayed by a week. They decide to try to get on an RAF flight
to Cairo, from where they can fly home to London, but there
is all the heavy luggage to sort out. Elisabeth treks to the
Jewish Belgian consulate, with the luggage and a note for a
colleague who is due to sail home the following week, asking
him to accompany their belongings; '…at last all was ready &
the Consulate freed of my lingerie'.

Even then, the journey is far from smooth. The first plane

they get on has hard seats and is extremely hot, and the next one has engine trouble and they are forced to find an alternative flight. Luckily they find two seats on a transport aircraft leaving a few hours later and, after a minor panic in which it is revealed that the British customs officers have lost their passports, they leave the Middle East, sputtering up through the clotted, dusty air and into the clouds.

*

Two things happen. My mother has a CT scan and this time it shows two new 'satellite' tumours in the same lung, and also shows that the main tumour is pinching her pulmonary aorta, reducing its capacity by 70 per cent. It is hard to reconcile this stark evidence of the progression of her disease with how healthy and fit she seems, but I have had a sense for the past few weeks that this has been coming. Something intangible in my mother's voice, her hesitation about going to the oncologist alone in case the news is bad, an almost imperceptible shift in the air. We have been waiting so long, and now I think it is finally here: the beginning of the end. The other thing that happens is that my stepfather is diagnosed with stage four melanoma, with metastases to his liver, spine and knee. There is no stage five.

Having already readjusted our projection of their future (Mum dead, him managing alone in their higgledy-piggledy old house, a widower for the second time), there is now an utterly blank space. My siblings, stepsiblings and I – there are six of us altogether – send emails to each other trying to grapple some sense from this news. We make plans for visits and think of practicalities. A list! We need a list! All the while I hold a hideous image in my head of my stepfather bedbound downstairs and my mother upstairs, both slowly and painfully fading away. This is my worst, my darkest thought, and this is what a diagnosis (two diagnoses) of incurable cancer is like: it is like walking along a rotten wooden bridge suspended over a raging river. You know the creaking planks will run out, you can see the emptiness in front, you can hear your fear crashing against the rocks, you may grasp at the scratchy rope edges – the clinical trials and genetically targeted therapies – but the swelling water thunders unstoppably beneath you.

There is, of course, a chance that my stepfather's cancer will respond to treatment, and that the slow-growing nature of my mother's cancer will mean she stays well for many more months. But I can't shake the feeling that we are all out of luck, that the inevitable turning has come and all will be lost.

And then there are the crows. First there are two, sitting in our garden, huge and menacing-blue. A few days later there are more in the trees and on the neighbouring roof, crawking as if demanding something. The week we first discovered that my mother had cancer again, I found a dead blackbird by my back door. I can't help but see these birds as harbingers of death, as symbols of the darkness to come. I begin to see crows everywhere. But these birds are also known in ancient cultures for other things – they are symbols of personal transformation, of magic, of prophetic insight and sixth sense, they are shape-shifters, and are considered by Hindus to be messengers from the world of ancestors. Perhaps I need to re-interpret these visitors. I have become quite good at this, turning away from thoughts of death, picking myself up and carrying on with my day, but something has changed and it is getting harder. I fear that, in Henry James' words, 'The wild waters are upon us now.'

9

Rio

Nu Xmas 1947	S. & C's stockings.	Nanny.	
Special list.	Marzipan animal.	Dragées.	
Bed-jacket or equiv.	Jig-saw	"Penguins".	
x Flannel	Crackers.	Mending things	C.
x Soap	Mascot enid.	Air-mail env.	
x Lotion	Small train	Shampoo	
Talcum powder	Playing cards	v Scissors	S.
? Face Rays	Coloured chalks	Large Sponge-bag	G.
x Scarf	Duster	Shopping-bag?	E
Razor ev.	Painting books.	g: Shoe-laces	C.
	Shuttlecock	Tie	S.
Diary	S: Watch	Dark glasses	C.
Writing things v	C: Car		
Dice			
Knitting		Toil-set.	E.J.
Biscuits	Sancha: Cardigan		
Cigs. & matches	José : Money & handkus?		
Ash-Tray			
Photos			

Henriqu. Mrs. Thomson. Burroughs?
Nurse at Hosp. Mrs. Mc.G.

When Gerry and Elisabeth reach London on 20 January 1947, after their exhausting journey back from Beirut, no one is expecting them. They are, once again, temporary residents, bunking down with friends and relatives, staying with Elisabeth's parents (now posted in Brussels), and preparing for the move to Brazil. There is an unrealness to this existence which must have been hard to process: two months after visiting the abominable woman coddling the pig for her charity ball, Elisabeth is back walking around London with a gurgling hot-water bottle stuffed inside her coat.

They leave for Brussels, and their awaiting children, at the start of February. From the luxury of the British embassy there, with its liveried footmen and marbled staircases, Elisabeth looks after the boys whilst Nanny is on holiday. Gerry returns to London and Elisabeth joins him on 28 February before he flies to Rio two days later. Elisabeth makes frenetic lists in the last few days before the move. Her descriptions of the garments to be packed – the gold hats and crocodile shoes – conjure up the razzle-dazzle side of her life. The prevalence of 'afternoon dresses' implies that this was to be a less demanding post, where Elisabeth would have lighter formal entertaining duties. She must have imagined herself promenading along the shore at Copacabana in her thin flowered frocks, her boys darting onto the sand, the smack of saltwater swims and the tropical air thick with moisture, a stark contrast to the arid land she had left behind just weeks before.

Elisabeth's lists show that her days over the next few weeks are spent packing, sorting and doing paperwork. She revises her choice of which clothes she will take to this new country, trying to gauge the meteorological and social climate. She and Gerry must slip, chameleon-like, into a new society. She will feel the familiar jangle of nerves and excitement. But there is something else contributing to these butterflies in her stomach. Around this time, Elisabeth writes in her diary of feeling 'bored not having enough to do, & feeling rather idle. Is it Miss Young?' She thinks she might be pregnant. Somewhere in the midst of all the packing and organising, probably during her and Gerry's brief reunion in London in February, my mother, Helen, was conceived. This is where she enters the story, and begins to add memories that enrich the tapestry of her mother's life I am weaving.

My mother has stuck a small pink post-it note on this page in the diary, obviously delighted to find herself here for the first time. There is a strange interplay between Elisabeth's hesitant question and the neon-pink note, my mother both here and not here.

Elisabeth sets off for Brazil on 19 April. The boys and Nanny will follow by sea two weeks later, on the *The Highland*

Brigade. It hasn't yet been confirmed, but Elisabeth is indeed in the early stages of pregnancy. She wears a label marked 'Rio' tied to her coat like an evacuee as she boards a small aeroplane. She is particularly anxious about the journey because the plane she was due to catch a week earlier (before her plans changed) crashed on landing in Dakar, killing all the passengers. She is seated next to an oversharing Brazilian woman, who speaks in very broken English, and her two small, unruly children. I imagine Elisabeth taking the list book out of her bag, flicking through the pages and pretending to be in the middle of something terribly important, just to avoid listening to the woman for a few minutes.

The flight is unpleasant. Elisabeth writes: 'I feel quite unreal in the air, & all the time half expect death…The noise of the engines gets on one's nerves after a bit, & anyhow sleep is difficult when one cannot lie down…I was alarmed by those funny little flames which appear to shoot off the wings.' To add to her anxiety, the plane is sent back to Lisbon due to fog and they have to wait before setting off again for Dakar.

Elisabeth notes that the airline food consists of stale meat covered in flies. The plane stops in Natal, on the northeastern tip of Brazil, where the passengers are sprayed with DDT (an anti-malarial measure, which now seems an appallingly toxic thing to spray on a pregnant woman) and have their temperatures taken. Three days later she arrives in Rio, exhausted and nauseous. I can't help comparing Elisabeth's austere, solo journey in the rickety plane with an account of one ambassadress, Lady Carlisle, arriving in Moscow in 1663 with her husband, her own carriage and two hundred sledges of luggage. Elisabeth and Gerry are quickly ensconced in a comfortable flat near the embassy chancery, with a sour-faced maid in pince-nez, and the boys and Nanny join them in May, following their seventeen-day sea voyage.

Elisabeth is unhappy in these early weeks, comparing the landscape unfavourably to the Middle East, complaining that Rio is mostly skyscrapers, and struggling to communicate her domestic arrangements in her limited Portuguese. In her diary she confesses, 'I always dislike places at first, and Rio is no exception.' She is also supressing a flickering fear that she will once more suffer the dreadful postnatal depression she experienced after the birth of her boys. This time she is far from home and will have nowhere to run to.

Yet she is gradually seduced by this lush country, the angular mountains rising in rocky juxtapositions behind the sea, the granite heft of the Sugarloaf Mountain puncturing the water and looking skyward towards the outstretched arms of the statue of Christ, the kaleidoscopic colours, the giant hydrangeas lining the roads, the stripes of the umbrellas on Copacabana beach, the roadside aviaries filled with parakeets and canaries, the vast swamps cut through by the heavy river, the papery blossom of the almond trees. She begins to keep cuttings of 'Crime in Brazil' from the newspapers, including headlines like 'Frigid Widow Shuns Swain, Carves Up Hapless Chap'. Slowly, tentatively, Elisabeth lets herself unfurl into her new home.

By the time she makes her list of presents for Christmas 1947, the family is properly settled. This is one of many Christmases they spend overseas, away from the traditional rituals of church, roast lunch, a walk and board games. This list shows how Elisabeth will recreate what she can of these traditions – the giving of stockings, and small presents for the family and Nanny. I love that she has put beside her own name that she would like a 'tool-set'.

And there is a new baby, my mother. I remember that my first Christmas with a newborn baby was spent at my mother's house, on our return from Australia. My son was only eight weeks old, not much more than my mother would have been for this Christmas in 1947 as her brothers unwrap their shuttlecocks, trains and painting books. We too had stockings that Christmas. As children, we would always pile into our parents' bedroom first thing on Christmas morning, clutching the bulging woollen shooting socks my father lent us for stockings. We had to wait until they had fetched a cup of tea before we tore into the gifts, amassing small piles of treats across their bed. Now my own children tumble into our room before dawn, flushed and chirruping. These traditions, as well as drinking bucks fizz for breakfast, having dollops of bread sauce and leaving the fug of the house for a bracing afternoon walk are all things that I have brought into my children's Christmases. Families assimilate rituals and find new space for their own. I wonder how many of ours were passed on from Elisabeth and Gerry.

I love this list for the connection it gives me to my mother's childhood Christmases, and the way it transports us immediately back to that post-war time of mending, hankies and jigsaws. At first I can't work out what kind of 'Penguins' Elisabeth was planning on giving Nanny, but then discover that Penguin biscuits were first produced in 1932, so it's likely that these and some sugared almonds were to be her gifts from Charles.

*

Brazil at this time is a democratic state, after years of political instability and dictatorship under a military junta. The country is a burgeoning nation on its own aspirational path towards becoming a major world power, keen to position itself as a major player in the Americas, capitalising on the post-war realignment of the political tectonic plates through the trade and exportation of valuable commodities like coffee, tobacco and sugar. Gerry and the British diplomats are aware of its strategic importance and the richness of its natural resources, and of the increasing attempts by the USA to woo the Brazilian government and people. It is a new world for Gerry and Elisabeth – a whole new continent. There is a thread here, though, joining the countries to which they have been sent – Spain, Lebanon, Brazil – each nation is attempting to pull itself forward towards better things out of the debris of war. Whether towards independence, totalitarian control, or superpower status, the countries in which my grandparents made their homes are on a trajectory and Elisabeth must navigate her own course through their landscapes and societies.

Rio de Janeiro has a flowering intellectual scene which espouses the tenets of Modernism, and the expansion of universities mirrors the new middle class's thirst for knowledge. There is also a flourishing women's movement, led by figures like the tenacious Eugênia Álvaro Moreyra, campaigning for women's suffrage. Hope seeps from the pores of the city and Elisabeth feels the prickling energy all around her.

Like the other places Elisabeth has lived, however, Brazil is divided and awash with inequality. Alongside a prosperous and growing middle class and an increasingly influential working class, the cities are home to migrants from poorer rural areas. This movement of workers to the urban areas marks the start of the *favelas*. Today's ubiquitous slum tenements that are home to thousands of Brazil's poor are beginning to dot the slopes of Rio, housing the incoming workers in search of jobs. In the decades before Gerry and Elisabeth arrive in Brazil, there were two waves of immigration from Europe, welcomed by some on the political right as a means of 'whitening' the nation, but resented by others as a form of colonial Europeanisation. Some factions are drawn to the ideas of fascism, and during the war the government dabbled with befriending the Nazi regime. An echo here of Franco's Spain, of Elisabeth having to confront a hateful ideology that continues to spread its gnarled fingers across the world even after Hitler has been defeated. In the post-war era, after the devastating persecution and destruction of Jews and other non-Aryan peoples, Brazil tries to paper over these undesirable political leanings. The country is a mosaic of races and it holds itself up as an example of the ideal of 'racial democracy', the ultimate melting pot.

Yet there are significant levels of inequality between white people and people of colour across the country, with disparities in education, wealth, life expectancy and employment.

In a country whose wealth was built on slavery, racist attitudes are simmering just below the surface. Buried beneath the Valengo dock in Rio de Janeiro (a landing stage where slaves were bought and sold until as late as 1888, when slavery was finally abolished) recent excavations have uncovered personal belongings and artefacts like jewellery and cowrie shells. It seems that, like the masks of Rio's famous Mardi Gras Carnival, behind the guise of prosperity and racial integration there is another, less appealing face.

Rio de Janeiro, the capital of Brazil until 1960 and Elisabeth's new home, is a city that arouses strong sentiment. Visiting in 1942, Orson Welles declared Rio to be 'at the end of civilisation, as we know it', while the writer Stefan Zweig writes: 'On the whole earth – and anyone having seen it once will agree with me – there is no more beautiful city, and it is unlikely that there exists one more unfathomable, more difficult to get to know.' It is a place that has inspired generations of artists, poets and writers, and provoked this impassioned reaction in an author whose book (produced in 1942) was filled with watercolour scenes from the area: 'Beaches, corniches, panoramas, forests, swamps, sand-bars…Rio…always Rio… This gives us the strange impression that we are exploring the curves, the salient, the hollows, the dark places and the dazzling beauties of some enormous giantess (like Baudelaire's), immense and beautiful before whom we kneel in tireless, insatiable adoration. Rio is a Woman-city.'

It was named after a non-existent river by travellers who believed the glorious bay must be fed by one source. Water is and always has been at the heart of the city: the generic name for the islands and settlements that first developed along the coast is *carioca*. Elisabeth learns that the word means 'child of the white man', 'white man's house', 'freshwater for sailors', or 'fortress', depending on the source, and if she asks for *carioca* in a restaurant she will be brought hot water. The waters surrounding Corcovado Mountain (the 'Hunchback') were believed to have magical powers, enhancing singers' voices and female beauty. These snippets of mysticism delight Elisabeth and add to the rich patina of Brazil's history, folding themselves into the story of this new country to which she must become accustomed.

Before quarries ripped into the hills, the physical line of the bay echoed the outline of Brazil, but by the time Elisabeth arrives, excavations and the repositioning of extracted soil to join the small islands have changed the landscape. It is a place where nature has at once defined and been shaped by human settlement, a place where water meets mountains, cotton-wood groves meet forests, and skyscrapers meet palatial hotels. In Elisabeth's time, it is home to around two million people, and is a desirable holiday destination for the inter-national wealthy set. The arc of a palm-lined avenue cups the busy harbour and miles of waterfront where people swim, sunbathe, indulge in water sports and promenade. A wide central highway cuts through the conurbation of high-rise buildings, Modernist buildings, churches, classical European buildings and tower blocks. Trams rattle along the teeming streets, with passengers hanging off the sides, and the pave-ments are inlaid with intricate tiled patterns and mosaics. For the brave, there is a precipitous cable car that glides slowly

The family, with Alethea and Nanny, at the top of Corcovado

up the slopes of the Sugarloaf; from the top the city looks like a stony growth clustering around a giant's hand. The statue of Christ stands atop Corcovado in celebration of how close the place is to God, arms outstretched as if to say, 'Look at this view! Look at the holiness of it, the sheer godly beauty!'

Everywhere in Brazil, but especially in Rio, there is a rhythm, as imperceptible as a heartbeat or as loud as the Carnival parade: it is the sultry, infectious sound of the bossa nova, the tango, the samba. It is a lush, juicy contrast to the Middle East – here women dance freely to this sexually charged music, all hips and heat and embraces. There is an easy sensuousness to life, the sounds, colours and movements rolling into each other. Elisabeth is won over.

*

My mother was born in November 1947, one morning when the household are eating their Sunday sausages. There is a photograph of her on a beach, aged about two, with Nanny and a large stuffed donkey, but she has no memories of her time in Rio. Before she was three my mother had crossed the Atlantic three times.

Thankfully, after my mother is born there is no sign of the dreadful depression that tore through Elisabeth's early months with her previous babies. She writes affectionately of her daughter: 'Helen was sick at 6, which caused a certain amount of havoc – but she continued to twinkle her very blue eyes, & to smile broadly. Her cheeks are so fat and pink; in fact she's fat all over, like an advertisement baby.' In her diary, she also notes details about her new baby that she may not have been able to take in fully with her first two in the midst of her depressions. For the first time, I get a sense of Elisabeth being a happy, confident mother: 'There are so many things about tiny babies that I find v pleasant: the gentle creaking noises they make when they are waking up in their cradles; their toothless smiles, & ecstatic kicking of legs & waving of arms with which they register delight; I like the vacant yet fixed way with which they gaze into space – or concentrate on their own toes or other neighbouring object. The back of their heads are very appealing: hair rubbed off, in places, but so soft and silky where it still grows. No necks, of course, just a fat wrinkle where their skulls end & their backs begin.'

This is poignant not just because Elisabeth is writing about my mother at the beginning of her life and I am watching her at the end of it, but because Elisabeth wouldn't see her daughter grow into a woman or become a mother herself.

She will not coo over her grandchildren, nor slip a coin into a soft small hand when they come to visit; she won't knit them rustic but charming jumpers, or breathe in their familiar sweet-milky smell and remember holding her own babies as an air-raid siren shattered the night or tropical rain spangled the streets.

Elisabeth's diary-keeping becomes erratic now, her time filled with children, household chores and being a diplomat's wife. There is an echo of times lost in one sentence she writes, recalling a more exotic life as she looks back through old engagement books: 'How odd it seems that 2 years ago our typical engagements were "Dine Jemil Bey", "Picnic Sa'adullah", "Party Khalil" & so on.' Whilst their time in Brazil is certainly less hectic and less sociable, it is not always easy. An ongoing water shortage means that water has to be brought in buckets and the children have to nip into the chancery wrapped in towels for their early morning baths. Washing, cooking and laundering is made more onerous. Typhoid has taken hold in the area and poses a real danger. But everyone in the family is enchanted by the country, in thrall to its vibrancy and pulse. Elisabeth describes the four days and nights of Carnival, watched by her boys who are equipped with paper hats, masks and streamers; and the fancy-dress ball Gerry attends dressed as a sheik wearing an *abba*, red shoes and one of my mother's nappies as a headdress, where he dances energetic sambas with scantily clad Brazilian girls singing some kind of 'umpah'.

During the summer months, the family move to Petrópolis, a town around seventy kilometres from Rio, set in a river valley in the hills of Serra dos Órgãos. Here the weather is warm all year round, and it is a popular summer retreat for Rio's richer inhabitants. Elisabeth and her children live in the ambassador's house and take their meals in the servant's bungalow, another temporary but well-liked home. Life is peaceful here, with mountain picnics where the boys chase frogs over waterfalls.

Another list, this one detailing items sent to the Petrópolis laundry, to be returned washed and pressed. They would be folded and put carefully away, checked off by Elisabeth as she reins in the reshaped, starched clutter of family life. In contrast to the lists of glass or clothes, this feels more private; it is an inventory of dirty laundry. There is a perfunctory, domestic feel to this practical list and it allows us behind the scenes, to stand alongside Elisabeth as she folds and puts away the pillowcases and towels.

An old friend of my mother's once told me that whenever he smells freshly washed linen he thinks of her. It was a funny thing to say but I knew what he meant. Staying in her house, in the attic room with sloping ceilings and handmade yellow curtains and hat boxes under the bed, you will always find crisply ironed sheets on the bed, and a jar of flowers from the garden on the bedside table. When I was young she used to ask me to help her fold the sheets, and I remember loving the firm flap we would give them as we held each end, the sheet billowing up and softly falling, then walking towards each other to fold it in half. She would take my two corners with a nimble pinch.

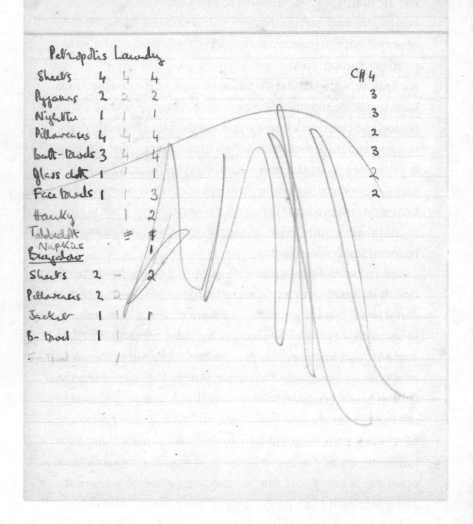

Petropolis Laundry

Sheets	4	4	4		CH 4
Pyjamas	2	2	2		3
Nightdress	1	1	1		3
Pillowcases	4	4	4		2
bath-towels	3	4	4		3
Glass cloth	1	1	1		2
Face towels	1	1	3		2
Hanky		1	2		
Tablecloth		≠	≠		
Napkins			1		

Bungalow

Sheets	2	—	2
Pillowcases	2	2	
Jacket	1	1	1
B-towel	1	1	
F-towel		1	

*

A storm is brewing across the yawning Guanabara Bay but the air is still and warm. Water-skiers slice across the waves and burnished swimmers plunge from the rocks on the other side of the road, making complicated eddies in a gently swelling lagoon. In the wolf-light Elisabeth sips an evening cocktail outside the flat as she watches people pass on their way to Copacabana. She has just got back from running errands (including delivering the ambassador's tortoise back to the residency in a Rolls Royce). She is well looked-after here. Nanny is a great help with the two boys and the baby and Gerry is mostly happy, despite feeling as if his posting is rather pointless so far from Europe.

Elisabeth's mind turns to the party she must organise. She picks up her book of lists and flicks back through her lists of other gatherings she has hosted, scanning the sherry parties, beer and sausage parties, fork dinners, soldiers' teas and buffet suppers for inspiration. She wants to arrange some music – perhaps that Hungarian accordionist, although wasn't there some *incident* at a previous party when he drunkenly assaulted a Portuguese maid? That same party when an inebriated colleague of Gerry's decided to walk home and went rambling off into the jungle by mistake. Maybe she will serve coconuts filled with *cachaça*, lime and sugar. A waxing splinter of a moon begins to rise over the bay, casting a faint yellow glow upon the water. Soon, for one exquisite hour, the Sugarloaf Mountain will turn purple in the dusk, before the colours of the bay retreat into the mid-grey mist. In the morning, the haze will shroud all but the tops of the crumpled mountains. The storm moves eastwards, over beyond Niterói and the twisted mangrove swamps.

*

In contrast to earlier lists outlining sumptuous food to be served at cocktail parties, this list from Rio in 1948 is entitled 'Simple Cooking'. It is a reflection of how Elisabeth's world has curled inwards, her family now her priority. This food is for them, and rather than constantly having to think about what the family is to eat, Elisabeth has made this list as a reference point. I'm not sure whether Gerry's addition of 'pigs' trotters' is a joke, but I love that he appears in this list (he seems to have added 'eel' too – perhaps a favourite?). Maybe they made it together, sitting over coffee and cake, discussing how to manage mealtimes, Gerry grabbing the pen once the list has been made and making his own suggestions.

The list is concerned with family life, not diplomacy. Gone are the days of frantic partying and carousing across Peking (though there is still room for Elisabeth to kick up her heels). Gone are the long, weary days of wartime domestic drudgery. Elisabeth can finally properly enjoy her children, and now that she is a confident hostess, she allows her role as a wife and mother to be her focus. There are, however, still demands on her time and the ever-present need to be the public face of British interests. In a city where bottles of whisky in boxes lined with satin are presented by shiny-faced businessmen keen to further the economic development of their nation, and the streets are regularly renamed to suit the political

Little Oaks:

Rio 1948   Simple Cooking.

Entrées, Fish, Eggs etc.   Meat.   Puddings

Eggs Florentines   Roast Lamb   Milk Puddings
Cheese Soufflé   Stuffed Loin of Pork   Fruit salad
Prawn pasties   Ham Roll   Fruit in Cream
Hors d'œuvres   Lamb cutlets   Lemon Sponge
Kedgeree   Sausages + Bacon } Mixed Apple Tart
(Chowderr Fish etc.)   Sauté Kidneys   } grill. Bread + Butter P.
Fried Fillets   Rolled Beef "or "Tracinho" Syrup Breads
Scotch Eggs (Steaks)   Croquettes   Jelly
Kedelbiac   Cornish Pasties   Banana Meringue
Fish + stuffing   Meat + Kidney Pie   Apple " (see over)
Club sandwiches etc.   Liver + Bacon   Lily's mousse
Vegetable stew + boiled rice Chicken + mushrooms
Eel.   Shepherd's Pie
Fish Salad
Shrimp Vol-au-vents   Tongue Milanaise
Petit Savins   Tripe   Liver Paste.
Smoked Salmon   Curry   Chicken's livers
Corn on the Cob   Presumada
Celery   Cold Meat + salads
Celery + apple salad.   K
                         Pigs Trotters.

agenda of whoever holds power, there are always deals to be done, alliances to build.

At the time, Argentinians joked that the Brazilians 'have dropped straight from their coconut palms into their Cadillacs', and this is indeed a commercial posting for Gerry rather than a political one. His work is primarily concerned with ensuring the stability of the country and pursuing Britain's economic interests. He feels left out of the post-war settlement negotiations and the restructuring of Europe, and is ready for a change.

The typhoid outbreak and water shortage contribute to Gerry and Elisabeth's decision to send the children back to England in the autumn of 1948. The family is due some leave for Christmas and so Nanny and the children (including my not-quite-one-year-old mother) are packed up and put aboard *The Highland Monarch*. Gerry and Elisabeth watch the ship sail past their verandah, just as it is getting dark, waving a white tablecloth wildly as their children disappear towards the open ocean beyond the Sugarloaf.

There is no firm plan for what will happen to the children once they get home, but Elisabeth and Gerry are not unduly concerned. They are used to last-minute arrangements and long-distance logistics. But matters are complicated somewhat by the Foreign Office suddenly cancelling Gerry's leave and saying that they are to be posted elsewhere instead. They pack their belongings into a van and await instructions. Gerry is having terrible problems with his legs (he injured them during a drunken dance and they have become septic) and Elisabeth is swamped by tedious forms about expenses

Helen and Charles on one of their Atlantic crossings

and pay: 'The "Inspectors" from the FO have arrived to go
into the matter of our pay. We have all been driven mad lately
by the forms we've had to fill in "in triplicate" & the ghastly
questions they ask. I seem to spend all of my time scribbling
calculations on the backs of old letters. Why should one be
asked to state how many times per annum we have our hair
washed & cut – & "If dyed, say so"? And how can we tell how
much we spend on feeding our domestic staff, as opposed to
"officer's own food"? G & I feel, our pay and allowances being
adequate, we would willingly sacrifice £100 p.a. <u>not</u> to have to
fill in the questionnaire.' This kind of bureaucracy is one of
the reasons why Elisabeth has become such a meticulous list
maker. Every few months during a posting, she has to account

for their outgoings, and there is a page in her book entitled, 'Details for Inspectors', which includes amounts for insurance, cutlery, children's clothes, cigarettes, drink, stationery and a book club.

The forms completed, Elisabeth and Gerry move into a hotel and finish their packing, once again not having any idea where they might be sent. They hold a farewell cocktail party and are given gifts of orchids and coconuts (not what you might consider essential items for a long sea voyage) and eventually set sail for England.

On 19 December 1948 Gerry and Elisabeth arrive home. They have problems with customs after Gerry fails to declare one small tin of tobacco – despite having a mighty customs list declaring 4,000 cigarettes and six bottles of whisky. They pay a £34 fine and set off for London. Outside their old flat in Holland Park, they self-consciously unpack a crate of cheese, meat and sugar in front of passers-by still suffering under rationing. Finally, they are reunited with their children, who have been staying at Elisabeth's parents' house in London, and Elisabeth describes how they were 'peeping round the curtains of the hall…They all seemed very well, & Helen much grown.' Nervous excitement on both the children's and Elisabeth's part, overwhelmed with relief at being together again, but with an edge of awkward shyness. This is their first 'proper' English Christmas as a family, with carol singers, church, stockings at 6 a.m. and a tree.

After Christmas, for a reason that I cannot discover, Gerry, Elisabeth and the children are sent back to Rio, not to a new post. Eventually, in January 1950, they leave Rio for good.

Despite the beauty of Brazil, Elisabeth is looking forward to scrubbing a kitchen back home, to the sullen skies and leafy damp of England. Their departure is straightforward and they are sent off with a fun farewell party, signposted 'Fiesta Young' along the road and attended by languorous Italian girls who close their eyes voluptuously during some of the songs, much to the consternation of the more conservative guests.

*

Reading Elisabeth's book of lists is a way of conjuring out of the dust and ink a person I never knew. Of course, my impression of her has been affected by the stories, photographs, diaries and other evocative sources we use to create an internal collage of a person. I find myself mourning the fact that I have none of my own memories of her and the objects she mentions. I can't look at the list of her clothes and think, 'There's the yellow scarf she wore to my wedding' because we never even met.

So the lists become a framework for my own version of Elisabeth. I imagine her standing – beautiful, tall and slender – at a fitting for her Chinese satin dress; or dusting and relining the drawers of one of the chests with pretty paper; or Gerry pulling on his tennis shoes and bounding across the grass. I imagine what it must have been like to have to count and keep track of all the linen and the glassware, as well as all the *stuff* that accompanies young children. The lists in her book were private, unintended for public consumption, and I am aware that in sharing them I am changing their place in the world – they are exposed, but also preserved. I am also changing the book of lists, bending the spine, rubbing away the cover, wearing away the paper by tiny increments. It is a fragile thing.

There is something I love about the materiality of the book itself, aside from the information it contains, something meaningful in the actual paper and card from which it is made. It is not just the familiarity and flashes of personality revealed by Elisabeth's handwriting, nor the fact that she held the book in her own hands and smoothed its pages; it is as though she has become part of it, as if she is still present. I wonder if tiny skin motes have remained lodged in the margins for all these years, and am reminded of the test tube purported to contain Thomas Edison's last breath, and the lock of Gerry's baby hair I found tucked into an old envelope. These talismans help us feel connected to the physicality of those who have passed before, giving us a tangible or at least containable piece of that person. This brittle, battered book still contains something of Elisabeth and it has begun to feel like an essential companion, something to protect me as we tick-tock forward through time.

Vladimir Nabokov once described how 'When we concentrate on a material object, whatever its situation, the very act of attention may lead to our involuntarily sinking into the history of that object.' This book is pulling me in, enabling me to sink into Elisabeth's story. But it is also keeping me afloat as my mother is slowly cast adrift. She is getting more tired, accepting offers of help she would previously have brushed aside, speaking less in large gatherings, turning down engagements. She comes to stay and we walk to my children's school and we stop so she can catch her breath. She is slowing down. She is offered radiotherapy to try to shrink the main tumour and make it easier for her to breathe. I go on with everyday life – cooking, taking my children to football matches, cleaning my house, working – but nothing feels real any more. I am going through the motions. I brace myself for a phone call. I want to be in Elisabeth's world, not my own.

When I first dipped into Elisabeth's book of lists she was a distant, exotic creature. But our relationship has changed. It is now something immediate, intense. I feel as if I am calling on Elisabeth for strength to deal with reality; I allow myself to feel things in relation to her that I don't know how to feel about my mother. Perhaps my attempts to reconstruct my grandmother are a rehearsal for when I have to remember my mother, after she is gone. A kind of deferred grieving – a loss-in-waiting.

10

Home

Garden-Party. The Fishery. June 9 1952

3 - 7 p.m.

Diplomatic Corps.

x2 Holvost	√ 2 Spanish Amb. + Duquesa P-di-R.	√ 2 Cortéverleys
x2 Côté	√ 1 Olivenes y Brugnera	x 2 Noel-Bakers
2 Crary-Chanel	x1 Cardi Arkana	1 Geoffrey Fisons
√2 Le Roy	2 Don Diego de.	√ 2 O' Duynes
√2 Lebel	2 Marquese de Lema	√ 4 Franklins
√2 Theodoli	x1 Don Jaime Alba	v 2 Hayward-Brown
√2 Farau	√ 2 Barneth	2 Thames
√2 Melasi - Ferretti	√ 2 Umbrulet	x 1 Stopford-Adams
√1 Toscanis Millo	√ 2 Squire Harris Row-Honses	√ 1 Edie Stopford
√2 Zecchi	√ 2 Penfield	√ 2 Harphams
x2 Abdul Nayed Handan	√ 1 Hulleys	x 2 Beaumonts
x2 Leb. Min. & Mlle. Khauis	x1 2 Achilles	x 2 Acton
2 Lux. Min & Amm. Clasen		x 1 David Acton
√2 Gevers	√ 10 Western Dept.	x 2 Beauhams
√1 Karnebeek	x 1 Miss Sully	v 2 Stokes
2 Schloch	x 1 Mrs. Clarke	x 1 O'Donnell
√2 Pole. Amb. + Senhora Ulrich	x1 Milo	√ 2 D'Arcy Gibsons
√1 Queinoy	2 Horves	√ 2 Wayland
√1 Patricio	√ 2 Christ/Jacks	

Total 107

Back in England in March 1950, Elisabeth, Gerry, the boys and my mother finally have somewhere they can call home. Following the death of his father, Gerry inherited the Fishery, his family's house near Maidenhead, Berkshire. Elisabeth's diary captures the glee of their first visit as the house's owners: 'The moment had arrived: G & I drove down to the Fishery, with our picnicking luggage, in the little Morris he bought at Aldridges yesterday.'

The house was built on the banks of the Thames, next to a small backwater with a wild, scrubby island in the middle. Gerry's family had moved there after a larger, grander house on a nearby island collapsed (due, apparently, to an over-ambitious and ill-thought-through plan to add an extra storey to the building). For over two hundred years, this stretch of the Thames had been home to generations of the Young family, an eccentric clan descended from an admiral. Their naval ancestry was reflected in the very fabric of the Fishery: the wood panelling in the hall was from the SS Mauritania, and the unusual double-forked staircase replicated a ship's stairs.

The Fishery

Like his father, Gerry grew up at the Fishery, and he inherited a love of water. The river was a significant presence in both his and my mother's childhoods. I find myself wondering what effect being so close to this constantly moving water had on those living there: the ever-present promise of adventure, of escape, of transition, of elsewhere.

For thousands of years, rivers have played a vital part in the story of humankind. We have thrown sacrificial offerings into them, created mythological creatures who live in their mysterious depths; they wash us, feed us, save us, entertain us, destroy us, flood us, irrigate our land, baptize us, drown us; we divert them, contain them, form fountains and ponds around them, harness them to generate power. My family is bound up in the story of this place; we have been shaped by it as well as shaping it, and a new generation now calls it home. As Gaston Bachelard writes, 'The anonymous water knows all

Gerry and a friend on a rope-swing over the river

my secrets. And the same memory issues from every spring.' This small stretch of the gently running Thames flowed through Gerry's and my mother's veins, connecting them to their home.

Elisabeth seldom writes in her diary from 1950 onwards, so I turn to my mother's memories and half-memories to conjure up their home. The original house was pulled down in the 1960s (replaced by a new house lived in first by my uncle and now his son), but my mother can remember all the rooms down to the tiniest detail. She walks me through it as she pictures it in her head. Over the front door there is a sinister stuffed armadillo, and to the left a morning room where she ate fish fingers for the first time. In the hall is a large music box. Behind this is a huge kitchen, with an Aga and scrubbed-pine table, and a scullery, larder and pantry off it. This is where they store the grand hampers sent by Elisabeth and Gerry's friend, the extraordinarily named Lord Talbot de Malahide and the Surrounding Seas. My mother remembers hunting in vain for Smarties amongst the *foie gras* in the baskets.

The dining room houses a large, formal table where Gerry and Elisabeth entertain, and there is a book-lined library which overlooks the garden and contains a sofa and comfy chairs. The family play board games and listen to music in the drawing room, which has French windows opening out onto a verandah. In the study, there is a cabinet full of shells collected by one of Gerry's ancestors (another one who was drawn to water). Upstairs are seven bedrooms. My mother's

Samuel, Charles and Helen with Elisabeth at the Fishery

room has wisteria growing round the windows and looks out on the river and the large garden. Chinese geese bob across the paddock, providing protection from burglars, and beyond the house is a garage where Gerry tinkers with old cars and builds kayaks. Further up the lane is a field rented to a market gardener, and attached to the house is a tenanted maisonette. My mother often visits the family living there, calling at 11 o'clock for a cup of cocoa and hunk of white bread ('Like Winnie the Pooh,' she says).

*

Something is crackling up in the plane tree. A woodpigeon bursts from the leaves. Across the river two small boys in matching corduroy shorts and tomato-coloured shirts dart out from under the drooping branches of the willows on the backwater island. Elisabeth calls them inside. It is getting dark, the mist spreading across the Thames and seeping into her skin. The air contains a chill note of autumn mingling with the mossy mud smells of the river. A delicate shroud of steam rises off the water and seems to be luring her to follow it upstream. She calls the boys again. They clamber down the bank into a small wooden boat, and begin rowing across to where their mother stands.

They all run up to the house together, the boys swinging their buckets full of today's catch (mussels, not to be eaten). Elisabeth holds the door open, grabbing the dripping buckets from the boys before they go inside. She glances across at the knotty roses, weighed down with their rain-bruised blooms, and makes a mental note to deadhead them tomorrow.

Whilst the boys go upstairs to get changed, Elisabeth helps Helen hang a painting she has brought home from school. The picture is of Gerry and Elisabeth going out to dinner, dressed in evening clothes. Helen used a new turquoise paint Mrs Plumridge had bought for the special bits, like the sash around Elisabeth's waist.

Gerry comes in from the side garden, where he has been busy with his latest project: turning the store room into a shed for growing mushrooms. He stamps the mud off his boots, leaning against the doorframe, and Elisabeth notices how well he looks. Flushed, alive, happy. She is content at the Fishery too, rooted, like the roses she tends, in the damp earth. She fetches some lardy cake from the pantry and the five of them eat it by the fire in the drawing room. Yes, she is finally home.

*

The family is posted overseas twice during the 1950s but this house is always the place they come back to. They are well known and well liked in the village, and Gerry enjoys attending church on Sundays and bellowing 'Ye sinners!' at the congregation (despite being ambivalent about religion). The boys are away at school, and Elisabeth and my mother are often alone here during the week. Elisabeth pursues the passion for gardening that began at Little Oaks during the war, writing in one of her diary entries: 'The garden is such a joy. Especially as it really is taking shape this year. The daffodils are just finishing, & tulips begin to come out. I have got so interested in it that I would willingly spend all day weeding.'

At weekends there are lunch guests, and the occasional party, but Elisabeth's life is mainly a domestic one. She writes about Chinese mirrors, lampshades and returning home early from a cocktail party in London to supper in bed brought by Gerry.

In 1953, they are sent to Rome. This time Elisabeth can leave their belongings safely at the Fishery, taking only what is needed. And she knows she can return. While on this posting, Gerry's drinking spirals into an obvious problem. The sheer quantities of alcohol sloshing about in all areas of diplomatic life are sweeping Gerry down a dangerous path. He nearly loses his job after turning up blind drunk to several functions and causing himself, and no doubt Elisabeth, great embarrassment. In 1955, they are sent back to England and Gerry is given a boring desk job back in London, which he hates but endures as a kind of penance for his poor behaviour. He writes that he had 'lost all the face there was to lose anyway long ago; so it's not too bad really'.

It is only after recognising that he is suffering from an illness and agreeing to undergo electroconvulsive therapy (ECT), that Gerry manages to give up drinking completely. ECT had become increasingly popular by the 1950s as a treatment for depression, schizophrenia, hysteria and 'sexual perversions', as well as for alcoholism. It was an aversion therapy, and a typical session for an alcoholic would involve the patient being presented with twelve test tubes of liquid, each of which they would have to sniff. Nine of the tubes would be filled with whisky and after sniffing these an electric shock would be administered. No muscle relaxants were given, and patients would experience violent full-body convulsions, which were designed to be as painful as the patient could bear.

There is a family story about Gerry jumping out of a car at some traffic lights on the way to a session of the loathsome ECT, and I am filled with sympathy for him, fleeing in terror from a brutal treatment that Ernest Hemingway described as 'frying the bacon'. (Hemingway shot himself just two days after a course of ECT.) Gerry must have lived in fear of a relapse and being forced to have more treatment, and I wonder what long-term damage the shocks may have done to his brain. Part of me feels there must be a link between this treatment and his later brain tumour, but although I find research showing evidence of brain damage and memory loss resulting from ECT, I don't find any connecting the treatment with cancer. Yet the feeling lingers, unnerving and unshakeable. Whatever the long-term effects, the treatment did put a permanent stop to Gerry's drinking, and he managed to recover his reputation and continue working for the Foreign Office.

Despite his troubles, Gerry remains a constant source of strength for Elisabeth, who is plagued by depression, often taking to bed for days at a time, unable to function normally. Again, although she is happy being at home, it seems that when there is stillness, without the need to present her best face, when she is quiet, she is less able to stave off the darkness in her head. Perhaps the effort and energy it took to maintain a diplomatic post also fed Elisabeth's spirit and held the worst effects of depression at bay. During these years, there is less activity, fewer lists, to channel her thoughts. When things are very bad, my mother is sent away from the Fishery, sometimes on a holiday with Alethea, or to Parham (where Elisabeth had found such solace). My mother remembers playing in a wood there, and sleeping in a twin-bedded room, a fluffy white dressing gown hanging on the back of the door and a plate of Digestive biscuits by the bed.

I get a sense from my mother's memories that she was often alone – not necessarily *lonely*, but alone, and self-contained. She plays with Boots (her beloved Dachshund), she rides, reads books in the large tree overlooking the island, plays tennis against a wall and pretends to be a librarian, classifying books with the organisational zeal she has inherited from Elisabeth. But her favourite pastime is messing about in boats, like her father.

One year, when the family is spending Christmas away from the Fishery, Gerry gives my mother a clue to the present that awaits her at home. She unwraps a matchbox containing one half of a walnut shell, and has to guess what it represents. The present turns out to be a boat: her own wooden dinghy, called *Dabchick*. Back at home she rows and rows, learning how to tie knots and speak the language of the river: whiff, skiff, clockheads, straiks, gunwale, tintles, clinker, cranky, wherry, shallop – the sounds of the words conjuring the slap and plash of the water, the noise of an oar skimming the surface or settling into the rowlocks.

Recently, at a loss as to what to buy my mother for what might be her last birthday, I bought her a voucher for an hour's boat hire in a nearby town. She rang me, joyous and childlike, from a boat in the middle of the river Avon. Later, she takes me to the same place and we row, taking it in turns, she by far

100 Sandwiches
& Biscuit Canapés { Loaves
Biscuits
Cream cheese & Olives
Hard-boiled Egg & Red Pepper
Cucumber & Radish
Shrimps

24 Bridge-rolls   Potted Meat.

50 Small Cakes

1-2 Big Cakes

Cheese straws ✓

Radishes
Nuts
Shrimps

Macaroons
~~Ginger bread~~

Potato crisps

Savoury puffs.

Notes : 60-70 people came.

Have 2 tables outside, &
another small one with food
etc. at other end of garden.
"One table for tea-urn, &
separate person to deal with
tea.
2-3 cut loaves of "canapés"

Amount of drink: 4-5 pints iced coffee.
Cup : 18 hock used
1 Brandy, 2 Rum, 1
Curaçao, 1 Gin, 1 Whisky.
If June 18-30   Best table

the stronger rower despite her illness, and I see the peace that being on the river gives her. On the water, we see the world at a different level, we move in a different way through the air; even time feels altered. As Elisabeth slips from this story, so my mother flows in, and I join her, rocking on the same eddies and currents, always moving.

*

This is one of the last lists in Elisabeth's book, although it isn't, exactly. There is no clear end to her lists, because the book is not a perfectly chronological record: the date on the facing page of this list is 1957, but on later pages there are lists dated 1947 or 1948. She switched between the pages of the book, finding the nearest convenient place to write, unconcerned with chronology and consecutiveness, simply needing a blank page on which to order her thoughts. In this lack of linearity and endings there is an important lesson for me. Elisabeth's book of lists doesn't have a clear finish – it is full up, certainly, but the lists loop back on themselves much as memories or dreams follow their own fluid timeframe. The list does not represent her last. But still, a cold dread slides closer like a draught. The pages of the book of lists are running out. With each leaf I turn, my time with Elisabeth is coming to a close.

This Garden Party list is similar to the other party lists Elisabeth made, but between the lines of the guests' names on the first page, the radishes, macaroons, iced coffee and bread loaves on the next, there is a farewell.

For once I can draw on memory rather than imagination to picture the location of the party Elisabeth is organising.

Although I never saw the original Fishery, I know the new house and its grounds well. I have spent many happy times on the same lawn where she placed two tables, and where she circulated amongst the guests, checking they had enough to drink, smiling and reassuring, glittering. The same trees that swayed above my children as they played cricket one summer on the grass would have shaded Elisabeth's guests. The walnut my mother planted on the lawn has grown into a large, strong tree.

Being in the water at the Fishery, on a summer holiday, I feel surrounded by these stories, as if the river is a material manifestation of my family's history. The poet Ted Hughes' advice to his son Nicholas was 'to live like a mighty river... live as though all your ancestors were living again through you'; it resonates deeply with what I have learned from this journey to find Elisabeth. I swim in the velvety cold, touching the cowbelly silt, feeling primordial weeds wrap themselves around me, each breath glancing onto the water and each stroke reinforcing the fact that I am merely a small part of something much bigger, much more significant. There will be sorrow, pain and things I can't imagine in store for us all, but there will also be love.

*

For Elisabeth 'home' meant a permanent retreat from diplomatic life, a place where she could tend the soil, be a mother and wife, decorate and furnish a house with her own possessions. We all need somewhere to belong. Sometimes this place is an imaginary construct, somewhere that exists as a vision of a place where life will be better, somewhere that is forever out of reach. We project our yearnings onto houses, pour our hearts into their bricks and mortar; they offer us an identity and a refuge, a psychic landscape. Sometimes a home and a person are so tangled up that they cannot be separated.

Elisabeth anchored herself in this house, and when she died the family home held an almost sacred place in my mother's heart. When the house was pulled down and replaced by the current building, she experienced a sharp sense of loss. She managed to keep the front door and put it into storage, but when she married and had a house of her own, she went back to reclaim the door, and found it had gone. I wish I could find it for her, but it has long since disappeared.

In the same way that we place stone upon stone and pour concrete into foundations to create a home, so we build ourselves from stories, fragments and scattered memories. The remembrance of the past allows us to create an identity. In his poem 'I Remember', Joe Brainard lists the minutiae of life which, taken as an isolated moment, mean little but which, read as a whole, form a life. After reading his poem I made one myself: a list of memories and scraps that had lurked unused and unacknowledged for years, but which have made me the person I am.

> I remember scraping my frozen dead guinea pig
> off the barn floor.
>
> I remember the feel of slimy pondweed slinking
> around my ankles.

I remember listening to Joan Jet and the Blackhearts.

I remember my mum making a crumble that tasted of paint.

I remember my friend Barry, whose dad painted the white lines on the roads.

I remember shaking uncontrollably.

I remember the smell of a horse on a hot day.

I remember running for the bus with my cello banging against my back.

I remember stealing from a charity collection box to get money for cigarettes.

I remember vomiting snakebite and black into the snow and it turning the snow purple.

I remember the strange way my mum pronounces 'éclair'.

I remember my first kiss with my first boyfriend, who tasted of cigars.

I remember spitting down onto my brother from the top bunk.

I remember the sound of bullfrogs in Bali.

I remember squashing a bee completely flat in the hinge of my bedroom window.

I remember my racist driving instructor.

I remember plucking my eyebrows for the first time in a hotel in Morocco.

I remember lusting after a yellow jumpsuit in
the C&A catalogue.

I remember the smell of my PE kit.

I remember having too-long gangly arms and
legs.

I remember finding two dead baby birds on the
pavement after I miscarried twins.

I remember my mum's voice before her cancer
came back.

This list of memories *is* me, in all its trivial, inconsequential mundanity. But memories are also deeply subjective, influenced by our senses as well as thoughts, beliefs and the meaning we assign to things. Memories can be false. Whether a witness wrongly identifying the perpetrator of a crime, or the brother who misappropriates memories that you know belong to you but he is sure happened to him, these fragments are fallible. Our memory decays over time, and our brain is constantly sifting information to decide what to save and what to discard. Forgetting is essential to allowing us to function, but for those things we need to remember, lists can be vital. Making a list provides a kind of external storage system for things that would otherwise take up essential brain space. In writing a list we are transferring some of the piles of mental clutter out of our head and onto paper (or a screen), leaving room for more essential or important information. The list becomes a paper version of the neurons in our brain which create an internal map and keep us located where we are. Oliver Sacks writes that 'The brain is an organism – which has to negotiate a complex world, from adequate representation of the world. To understand the world – to see or make meanings – to categorize.'

As I search through piles of old photographs, themselves records of memories, I spot Elisabeth's sister's shaky handwriting on the back of some. Alethea has scrawled questions like 'Who was she?', 'Minaret, but where?' and 'What have I got in my hair?' (she has mistaken a rip in one layer of the paper for a peculiar floral headdress). It is as if she needs these pictures as prompts for her memories, but finds them failing, too distant, the past slipping vertiginously away as she gets older and older. Yet she has now become part of the memory, of the moment captured in furry black and white – every time we see the picture we will see her holding it in her tiny withered hands, propped on an institutional pillow, baffled by the world, alone.

A web of memories – full of gaps and patched over with imagination – holds us together, the filaments binding us into a family unit and giving meaning to our existence. As Virginia Woolf writes: 'Memory is the seamstress, and a capricious one at that. Memory runs her needle in and out, up and down, hither and thither.' It is not just blood that makes us kin, but this spidery silk of threaded memory.

At times, I wonder if my search for Elisabeth is purely escapist, taking me further away from the person I need to be to deal with what lies ahead. But I come across some research at Emery University which finds a correlation between the depth of knowledge of a family's history and the ability to cope with hardships and feel in control of one's own life. Nostalgia – story – builds identity, adding to the layers of memories we have laid down for ourselves and linking us indelibly with our forebears. And at this moment it is exactly what I need. I hold on to the thread.

11

Paris

Write to

Nancy Brown   37 William St. Herne Bay Kent

Cousin Cicely	3 Belgrave Place S.W.1.
Vicky	R.A.F. Hosp. Matlock, Derbyshire.
Anne	Silver Birch, Plantation Road, Leighton Buzzard.
Diana	78 Prince George Av. Southgate N.14
Betty	Fernhurst Rise Haslemere.
S-Adams	Bawdsey, Bletton Road Gerrards Cross.
Cousins	122 Iver Court, Baker St.
Diana	~~Vic.~~ Vic.2360 Exr. 186
Hopes	Ewell 2109
Dr. Kemp –	Upholsterer of Sofa etc. 46 Alliston Road, N.W.8.
Twin.	7 Tedworth Sq. S.W.7
Prestedge	3 Hereward Sq. Ray. 1308, 1913, 1939.
	('6 Francis)
Shaws	50 Hanover Street Ken. Vicky, Paul
Betty Barlow	Rand Ho. Northampton

WHEN ELISABETH ANNOUNCES THAT THE FAMILY IS TO move to Paris, my mother (now aged eight) shuts herself in her bedroom for the rest of the day and refuses to come out. Her brothers are both at boarding school by now, so they will stay in England, but Nanny is to go with Elisabeth, Gerry and my mother. She hates the idea of leaving her beloved home and her dog. But, inevitably, the move happens. After a few weeks staying with Elisabeth's parents at the house in Kent to which they have retired, my mother joins Elisabeth and Gerry in Paris in April 1956.

There is less material for me to draw upon now. Elisabeth's diaries have petered out, the book of lists is full. She is slipping from my sight. But I do have fragments that my mother remembers, and from these I must piece together the last months of Elisabeth's life.

Gerry must have redeemed himself in the eyes of the Foreign Office, as Paris is a coveted posting for British diplomats. There are concerns amongst the British establishment that the French will fall prey to the perceived evils of Communism, so the British diplomats are there to ensure the

Elisabeth and Gerry in full regalia at the Paris embassy

country resists undue influence from radicalism. The family live in a tall, elegant house on Avenue Théophile Gautier, where Elisabeth busies herself with the usual round of house-hold chores and diplomatic hostessing. My mother is sent to a progressive school, along with several other foreign diplo-mats' children, which she enjoys, despite the initial language barrier. When she arrives, she is asked if she would like to join the children '*dans la forêt pour cueillir des jacinthes sauvages*', but as she thinks this means hunting for wild animals (which, for all she knows, is how French schoolchildren spend their time), she declines. But she settles in and makes friends. On Thursdays she goes ice skating and on Sundays the family go for picnics by the river at the Château de Dampierre. They return to England and the Fishery for short holidays and some official entertaining, but Paris is now their base.

They have not been in France long when Elisabeth becomes ill. At first everyone thinks she is suffering from exhaustion (from the stress of the move and a new post), and it is agreed she can take a year off from diplomatic duties to recover if necessary. Her depression has returned. Gland trouble is suspected. Blood tests are done. In the early summer of 1957 she travels to England to stay in a nursing home in Wimbledon while doctors work out what is going wrong. At the back of her book of lists is a record of addresses, added to and amended over the years, and now a vital source of information for communicating with her friends. She did not tell many people that she was ill, but it would have been reassuring to her to know that this central reference point was there in case she needed to contact anyone. Her closest friends come to see her, but as this was thought to be another bout of depression, they are not summoned for emergency visits. The collection of people in this list is at once random and at the same time encapsulates Elisabeth's life in England: dear friends, an upholsterer, cousins.

Gerry writes loving and encouraging letters to her from Paris, including humorous titbits from embassy life that he thinks she will like: 'Mme Norstad was making her first appearance after having been crippled for life by a machine into which she had strapped her bottom with a view to reducing it. A tragic but not unfunny story, I thought.'

His letters become increasingly frustrated as he tries to glean information at a distance. I have no first-hand accounts from Elisabeth, no diaries or lists to go on, so my position feels similar to Gerry's. Gerry pleads with Elisabeth to concentrate on getting her body better and to believe that once the illness is gone, her mind will also recover. It seems the doctors are more inclined to see Elisabeth's illness as a manifestation of a mental disorder, which Gerry fiercely disputes: 'When you left Paris there was something, or a variety of things, <u>physically</u> wrong with you. What these are we shall learn in the next thrilling installation. And then we shall get the damned thing licked.' There are worries about her lungs, talk of fibrosis. After two weeks apart, he arranges to come to England to see her. He will bring some of Elisabeth's belongings, and hands over the responsibility for list-making to Nanny (whom he refers to as Norris): 'Betty is looking forward to packing your things, and I'm sure Norris is as handy with a list as you are – or nearly.' Her lists have not gone unnoticed all these years. I feel another lovely connection with Gerry here, both he and I loving Elisabeth for her list-making habit.

On 8 July 1957 Gerry returns to Paris, leaving Elisabeth behind. He is still writing to her of the future, yet I can't help but wonder if he knows by now that she is dying and just wants to hide it from her as long as he can. One heartbreaking letter says: 'If I could be converted into a nourishing soup for you nothing could give me greater pleasure.' His letters reveal uncertainty about what is to come: 'And I think this admirable intertwining, if inhibited, love of ours you tell me of will survive physical separations all right... And try not to fret about plans. They really are all quite safe with me & mine.' 'Meanwhile just tell yourself over and over again that you've nothing to worry about; that everybody loves you.' 'I try to send you waves of love over the ether, & hope that some of them impact. If you feel your ear twitching it'll be me kissing it.'

Perhaps Elisabeth makes some more lists – possibly of appointments Gerry must keep, household supplies, things my mother needs for school, anything else she can think of that will help her children and husband manage without her for the time being. I am not sure whether Elisabeth is aware of just how ill she is. Maybe she knows she is dying but doesn't tell anyone; maybe they are keeping it from her in order to protect her. I do know that not once in any of the letters does anyone mention the word cancer. I find a picture online of the doctor who was treating her and I am filled with fury and sadness on seeing his face. Here were the eyes that tried to see into hers, this was the mouth that spoke to Elisabeth of her chest, her corpuscles and her mind, but *why didn't he save her*? I can only imagine the impotence and rage Gerry must have felt.

In the end, no matter how much we strive to grapple our thoughts and possessions onto paper, our lists cannot keep death away. Lists that were framed with love become coloured by loss.

Elisabeth dies in hospital in Westminster on 16 August 1957. My mother, aged nine, is on holiday in Cornwall with Nanny and Alethea, who gives her the news. She returns to their home in Berkshire, to the bedroom with wisteria around the window, but nothing is the same. She escapes into the Agatha Christie book she is reading. Gerry meets his eldest son off the train in London, on his way from school to visit his mother, greeting him with the words, 'She's gone.' The worst thing that could possibly happen to these children has happened. After Elisabeth's funeral, the children are sent to Scotland to stay with friends, and my mother returns to Paris soon after, with Nanny. She becomes very attached to her old dolls, taking them everywhere, acting out the role of the mother she has lost.

*

Elisabeth's death certificate. I ordered this flimsy piece of paper and when it arrives I am floored. For as long as I can remember, we have been told that Elisabeth died from lung cancer, the same cancer my mother now has. But here the stated cause of death is different: 1) broncho-pneumonia 2) intestinal carcinoma 3) carcinomatosis. The primary cause of death is the same as that on her brother Norton's death certificate, a horrible mirroring of ends arrived at in very different ways. Pneumonia is deadly in those whose immune system has been weakened by chemotherapy or radiotherapy, or those who have tumours in their lungs, so it would seem Elisabeth had a secondary infection in her lungs that precipitated her death. Carcinomatosis is the term medics use when epithelial cancer has spread to many areas of the body. Elisabeth was riddled with it. Intestinal carcinoma would now be called bowel cancer, and this is where I am shocked. My mother had bowel cancer in her forties, her mother died young from it – what then for my generation? I have just passed forty-two, the age Elisabeth was when she died. Now I discover there is a strong line of hereditary cancer in the female side of my family.

I contact a family-history medical unit who ask for detailed notes and we create a rather grisly family tree, with notations for all those who had cancer and who died from it. My mother goes for blood tests and we are told there is a chance she carries a particular genetic mutation that means her children will have a greatly increased risk of certain cancers. I consider whether I would have a preventative hysterectomy and I make an appointment for a colonoscopy. When we discover, some months later, that they haven't found a marker for that genetic syndrome, I am relieved, but not off the hook. Something has shown up in my mother's genes but they are not sure what it is yet.

It is possible that Elisabeth also had a genetic predisposition to certain cancers and she passed this on to my mother. This does not automatically mean that I am at greater risk, but it all points to the need for vigilance. I will not live cowed in the shadow of this disease that has caused such damage and loss in my family, but I will be prepared to face it down if it comes. In my most lost moments, I become convinced that my search for Elisabeth was always meant to happen, that the book of lists was supposed to lead me to this death certificate, that it will save my (or my siblings', or my children's) life.

*

I decide I need to go to Paris – I have been several times, but not since uncovering Elisabeth's lists and beginning to rebuild her life. This is the last city in which Elisabeth and Gerry lived together, and to which she never returned. It is also the place where Gerry died. I ask my mother to come with me.

I contact the British embassy there, struck by the idea of taking my mother back, perhaps for the last time, and they agree to show us around. Along with my two eldest sons and my mother I catch the Eurostar, barrelling through Kent at dawn on a blindingly bright morning. Once in Paris, we spend several hours doing touristy things and then head to the embassy. The building was originally a palace. It is an opulent, regal, extravagant place, set back from the road and guarded with a chain and a stern-looking soldier. An image flies into my head: Elisabeth's two young boys in Brazil, running to the embassy chancery wrapped in towels to have their baths. I can't imagine such mischief happening here. We cross the imposing courtyard and are met by a friendly woman with whom I have been exchanging emails. I can see my mother drinking it all in, dragging the memories from so long ago back to the forefront of her mind, slipping back to her days in the embassy garden, to the secret doorways and passages only children can know.

The rooms are impressively grand. My mother remembers Elisabeth going for dress fittings in preparation for a visit by the queen, but perhaps she never wore the garments, as she became ill so soon after they moved to Paris. I wonder if the beautiful Dior dress that I now have was from one of these fittings.

This photograph of Elisabeth – labelled 'The Last Photograph', and kept carefully by Gerry in a card frame and covered with tissue paper – must have been taken here. She is sitting at a dinner, surrounded by older men in military uniforms and smart suits. There is a slick of grey across her

Elisabeth at a Paris dinner party

waved hair and she is wearing a strapless gown that reveals her thin chest, within which was growing, unbeknownst to anyone, a tumour. One of many spreading through her body. She is looking at the man next to her, who is clearly enjoying their conversation, but her gaze is thrown just beyond him, into nowhere. One of her hands twists a spoon on the table. She died just two months after this dinner. She must have been feeling so awful, rattled with wheezes, tired deep within her bones, darkness in her head. Yet there she is, performing her duty.

We are shown around the gold and chintz of the formal reception rooms by a charming butler (my boys can't believe they have met an actual, real-life butler). We walk through the gardens, and look for the window from which Gerry would have watched my mother as she played amongst the roses and tall hedges. Eventually we leave in search of ice cream and the family's apartment building, not far from the embassy's wide avenue. The Avenue Théophile Gautier is surprisingly quiet, so near to the hurly-burly of central Paris. Plane trees shade the tall townhouses set back from the road. My mother isn't quite sure which was their house, but she thinks she spots it on the right, an elegant building with balconies and lofty views. It was all such a long time ago. And the boys are grumbling now, keen to find food, so we don't linger as long as my mother might have liked.

Lying in my hotel bed later, listening to the rumbling city outside, I churn over images of Elisabeth in Paris (some real, some imagined). I realise that it is all here, in this place: the beauty, the glamour, the toil and the sadness of Elisabeth's life. My mother lies in the room next door trying to sleep, and I wonder if this visit has healed something in her, or whether all this revisiting of the past will just cause her pain. We have talked a lot about my research and she is delighted that I am telling Elisabeth's story. Sometimes I find out things she never knew, and sometimes I need her to clarify events or timelines. In the moments when I wonder if it is wrong to be exposing the intimate details of Elisabeth's life in this way, her enthusiasm and approval spur me on. I am writing this as much for her as for myself. I am struck afresh by the unbearable emptiness the deaths of her parents must have left.

*

After Elisabeth's death, Gerry's sister Joan, who shared Little Oaks with them during the war and is now a widow, moves into the house on Avenue Théophile Gautier, with her two children. Gerry is an affectionate father, telling my mother to 'be happy and then be good, in that order'. He does his best to get on with life, with the gaping loss always at his side. It is as if part of him has been cleaved away, leaving raw flesh and exposed bones. Sometimes he feels he can't go on with his job without Elisabeth. It is unthinkable that life should carry on. But for three years it does.

Gerry keeps the many condolence letters written to him, connecting him to the wife he has lost, enabling him to remember her as she was when she was well. Some are from people mentioned in her list of addresses, shocked and confused by her death. One friend writes: 'To know Elisabeth was to laugh with her, and to laugh with her was pure joy. She

had a most infectious gaiety & enthusiasm for all she under-
took…and I have heard her, by some witty chance remark,
turn the right way up again a world which to a dispirited
listener had seemed full of sadness and despair. She had the
knack of making the discouraged feel that life was full of
interest and delight.'

*

There is another folder of condolence letters. These were
written to Gerry's sister after his death in 1960. In early
March, he is taken ill and, despite the pills he takes under the
diligent watch of his sister, his condition quickly deteriorates.
He has a brain tumour. There is little record of his illness, but
he may have suffered symptoms such as headaches, nausea,
depression, drowsiness, irritability, changes to his vision,
confusion, short-term memory loss (some of his letters to my
mother do mention his forgetfulness) and problems walking.
Again, it is frustrating to have so little information, but I can
only hope that Gerry was not aware of how serious his condition was, that he didn't sit alone, racked with agonising fear
and concern for his children, terrified of what would happen
to them if he died.

Following complications arising from surgery to remove
the tumour, he died on 17 March: Elisabeth's birthday. Her
brother had died on their father's birthday, and I wonder about
the significance of this. But death doesn't always happen on
one day or in one instant – it is a process, parts of the body
fail in their own time, memories and the sense of who we are
drift away before we are pronounced clinically dead. I don't

know when Gerry began dying, but I do know how his death felt for my mother.

She was aged twelve and at boarding school in England. She has been writing regular letters to Gerry, full of pleas for a pony or news of reaching the semi-finals in a ping-pong tournament. In her diary at the beginning of March, she writes: 'Cried because Daddy's got jaundice and Sister said people hardly ever die of it. But that's not much consolation. He CAN'T die and leave me all alone, God wouldn't let him. Oh God, PLEASE don't.' On 13 March, she writes: 'Felt v. miserable because Daddy's just been operated on his head. Nanny rang up in breakfast. Daddy you MUST get better, what shall I do if you don't? Felt v. worried. Oh God you mustn't kill him, you mustn't.' Then: 'Ally [Alethea] took me away from school, because Daddy died in his sleep last night. I'm trying not to cry, as it will be such a heavenly birthday present for Mummy. And they'll be together, which is what they wanted. Now I'm an orphan and we're poor. Au revoir Daddy.'

The tributes to Gerry are a testament to the man he was: charming, kind, helpful, honourable, brilliant, modest. Some letters refer to the 'tragedies that lay in store' for him, 'how cruelly life has treated him', how maybe he is happier now. One letter includes this comment: 'I felt his gallantry and respected his courage and his style of being. Being with him always made me feel happy and I loved to look at his dear, quizzical face. I shall miss him very much. And I know that I am the richer for having been his friend.' Reading these letters and diaries is almost unbearably painful. All the sorrow I have felt for Elisabeth and Gerry, for my mother and her brothers losing both their parents, floods over me. I can't comprehend what this loss means, how my mother can still have faith in the God who ignored her begging for her father's life. I question whether I should even be reading these documents that are soaked in such sadness, but I *can't* just put them away, close the files and stuff them back into the battered old suitcase they have lived in for so many years. Elisabeth's story has become my story and I can no more turn away than I can turn inside out. I write on, because, as Hilary Mantel asks, 'What is to be done with the lost, the dead, but <u>write</u> them into being?'

*

For the rest of her childhood, my mother was looked after by a combination of kind aunts, and lived mostly at the Fishery. The house became a container for her loss, a place she could feel the presence of her parents and relive her happier memories. The heartbeat of the house steadied her. I recall these lines from John Donne:

> Yet nothing can to nothing fall,
> Nor any place be empty quite.

Although the old house no longer stands, the land, the river, the trees all hold these people who once lived there. This place will always be 'home' for my mother, for my cousins and now for their children who live in the new house, building their own set of memories, etching their mark on the trees and kayaking along the backwater. Elisabeth lives on through these new generations; the love she had for her children is the same as the love I have for mine and for my mother. Love remains and will always remain, regardless of the shifting bricks and slates of buildings; it runs in the river and in our blood. It is extraordinary yet true that you can love a person you never knew, that you can feel connected by something greater than breath and heartbeats. Elisabeth's book of lists has brought me here, to this spot by a river, preparing myself to say goodbye to my mother but knowing that she too will live on.

*

A while ago my mother wrote me a list of her own: a list of memories of Elisabeth. It is a touchingly simple list, a life contained within a few lines, a child's most significant relationship condensed into these scattered fragments. In this list, my mother is refracted. I see her as a young girl, backlit by the golden glow of nostalgia, holding her hand to her eyes, searching into the sun, a shadow spilling behind her. Here is what she wrote:

Memories of my mother

I'm often shocked at how few memories of my mother I can consciously summon up. I really don't know how this part of my memory works, but I wish it worked better.

Here are some, in no logical order.

In the bathroom, shaving her legs and I think painting her toenails.

Same place, crossly scrubbing me in the bath
with Vim because I had painted myself like a Red
Indian and it wouldn't come off.

Helping me put my socks on ready for school.

Sitting on the stairs to use the upstairs
telephone to ring up Mrs Plumridge's, the little
school that my brother had been to, to ask if I
could start right away. This was after we came
home from Rome, and I was about 5.

Cooking apple sponge, which we called
'Saturday Pudding' because we had it on
Saturdays.

Giving me fish fingers for the first time ever –
I think they had only just been invented.

Sitting with me after school, eating lardy cake in
the drawing room by the fire.

Being understanding but firm when I refused
to eat vegetables – I must have been about 8 or
9 – and getting in touch with the school to try to
reach some compromise about my fussiness.

Me walking with her to the car, skipping as
I went, before she drove me to school.

Her wearing a pink pleated summer dress, with
the pink getting darker as it went down to the
hem. She looked absolutely beautiful in it.

Lots of commotion when they had a huge garden party one summer.

Her lying in bed not seeming to do anything, and me being sent away to stay with cousins. I think this was a depression time.

Her laughter.

Her listening to *La Mer*, a French song my brother recently gave me a CD of.

Her ringing the butcher on Fridays with the order for the weekend meat, which he delivered.

'Helping' her in the garden, sometimes weeding with Alethea, who came down lots of weekends.

Her being very sweet and kind to me when we had lunch in the Copper Kettle (a cafe in the High St) when I was being very fussy about my food and some women sitting nearby said, 'Won't eat this, won't eat that – the child ought to be spanked.'

Going with her to Budgens to do the shopping. We stood or sat at the counter reading out the list and shop assistants bustled around collecting all the things.

Her kissing me goodnight before they went off to watch a tennis match.

Her and my father in the bathroom, which
had huge mirrors everywhere, and she would
wallow in the bath while he shaved and put nice-
smelling stuff on his hair.

My picture of her is a hazy beautiful perfect
almost supernatural person whom I adored, but
who seems in my memory up above me rather
than close next to me.

EPILOGUE

For the four days that we are camped at the hospice, time becomes elastic. We (my brother, sister and I) sleep in shifts for an hour or two, then return to our mother's bedside. It reminds me of having a newborn baby, this blending of day and night, the endless murmuring hours of nothing much happening except the most important thing of all.

Then the doctors take me into the 'Quiet Room'. I know this can't be good. They tell me softly that they have been unable to control her symptoms and that she has 'short days' left. I leave the room and feel I am suspended in time, as if that was the longest conversation I will ever have, yet it was over in minutes. I make calls, cry, sneak into the staff-only kitchen to make tea, sit in the garden and watch younger and less fortunate people than my mother eke out their last days in the sunshine. A man is planting geraniums in some pots. We chat about gardening and his previous job and all I want to do is howl at the trees.

It began two weeks earlier when my mother returned from a holiday in Greece. She was unable to keep food down, choking and vomiting into the gutters. I drive to her house to meet her and my stepfather when they get back from the trip, feeling that this is the beginning of the end. Over the next few days she quickly gets worse. We take turns visiting, ordering more cardboard sick bowls (which she calls 'top hats' because of their jaunty shape), puréeing food that will moments later be spewed back up, talking, washing her thinning hair (how strange and moving it is to touch her like this, our roles reversed), folding her clothes, explaining things to various doctors, clutching at solid surfaces to steady ourselves.

When I am back at home I feel a compulsion to be in cold water, jolting my body out of its grief with the sting, buoyed by the luminescent pool so that I don't have to keep myself up. As I swim my breath becomes the sound of my mother's breath, willing her with each exhalation to keep going, to get better, but knowing that this is not what will happen. The water cradles my body and my breath melts into the sound of the liquid around me and I offer it up to the sky in some kind of prayer.

We can't cope; she needs more help than we can provide. She goes into the hospice for 'symptom management'. After a couple of bad nights, she is given a room to herself, filled with flowers and medical paraphernalia, a CD player and a copy of *Little Dorrit* on her bedside cabinet. We show visitors in, find jars for their roses and then sit outside while they say their goodbyes. Each time it gets harder to watch. Her brother brings her a branch from the walnut tree that she planted as a girl at the Fishery. I twist off the nut from the branch and tuck it into my bag, planning to plant it somewhere.

Sometimes we laugh. My mother asks us to make a list

(of course!) of all the holidays we went on as a family, which prompts funny memories (an evening in Brittany when everyone accidentally got very drunk on *eau de vie*; our own version of the Olympics in Scotland, including jellyfish-catching; trying to attract bats in Italy by throwing socks with stones inside up in the air). This year, I stopped dyeing my hair, cut it all off into a short, grey pixie cut, very like my mother's. A slightly dippy nurse mistakes me for her sister, which I find rather galling, but we giggle at her attempts to cover up her error, and I worry that, when I am lying in the spare bed in my mother's room, a nurse might mistakenly try to give me an injection or turn me over. One time my mother wakes up from one of her more-frequent naps, woozy with morphine, and says, 'Oh, I slept like a launderette.' We laugh as she remembers trying to get high on Davidoff (we aren't sure what this was) with her best friend when they were teenagers. Sometimes she says random things, like 'Eggs!' and we exchange bemused glances, asking if her legs are hurting, or does she want some scrambled eggs. She seems to be slipping in and out of our world, her mind groggy and slowing.

She talks about dreaming she is beside a lake and later of walking along a road. My last conversation with her is about Elisabeth and Gerry. She tells me, 'You are my Elisabeth,' and I don't understand what this means. I don't believe in the afterlife but am suddenly desperate to cling to some sense of continuity. She believes she will see her mother again, and I can't accept that I never will.

Unable to process food or water and as the cancer takes hold, she slowly slides into unconsciousness, lulled by music and the prayers of her friends. There is a smell that pervades the room, the smell of something rotting. Of death, I suppose. It gets into our mouths, and no matter how furiously I brush my teeth I can still taste it. I feel like I am breathing death. A fly circles for a whole day and night, waiting for the carrion. We become accustomed to a background soundtrack of the whir, thrum and click of the oxygen machine, of our mother's gasping breaths, leaves rattling in the trees outside her window and the medical sounds of the building around us.

She is calm and not in pain. Her frail body makes sharp contours in the sheets where her bones are protruding. Like the hull of a boat, all ribs and skin, curved so it can make its way smoothly across the water to another place, without us. The skin on her hands and feet begins to turn a mottled purple. I have read about this. It won't be long now.

The last night there are a couple of moments when, sitting with her, watching and waiting, holding her hands and letting our tears drop onto the metal bars of the bed, we think she has died. But then her breathing starts again. Rasping but dry, not the foaming bile that has frothed from her mouth over the last week.

My sister thinks we should ask the hospice chaplain to come and say some prayers. I am not in the room, I am lying in the hospice's family flat, trying to work out why someone who is so ready to die just doesn't seem to be letting go. We have all said she should go whenever she is ready, that we will be OK. I had heard that this is what people need sometimes. But still, her chest rises and falls, her body immobile except for this shallow rhythm. The chaplain says some prayers, and something shifts in the room and my sister feels her relax. Her breathing slows. They call my brother and me into the room, then leave us to say goodbye. It is all just as she wanted, and she is surrounded by love.

She looks serene, peaceful, beautiful. Her last breath is barely perceptible. But it is obviously the last.

*

And now, sitting in a cottage in the Lake District one month later, I am left trying to make sense of the unfathomable reality that I will never see her, speak to her or hear her voice again. I had thought I would feel her presence, as I have felt Elisabeth alongside me, but until now there has been nothing. I am splintered, tattered, yet wading in the moil of loss I mostly feel numb. I couldn't save her; this book has failed to save her. Every time something good happens I think, 'I'll have to tell Mum,' and then remember all over again. The first weeks after her death I dream that I am still by her bedside but have fallen asleep, and I wake up gasping. People seem to avoid me in the street, as if they can smell my grief. I feel like I am coated in a meniscus of sorrow – an afterdeath.

She has been here, to this cottage, and I lie in bed thinking of her breath falling on these pillows as the morning light slides down from the fell. Every time I catch my reflection it reminds me of what I have lost, my hair so much more like hers, and I regret cutting it off. My sun-toasted, freckled arms look like hers lying lifeless on the hospice blanket. I am haunting myself.

As I sit one morning on the doorstep, looking over the

fields to the milky lake and the scree-encrusted mountain beyond, I feel a change in the air. A tiny robin lands on the wall about six feet from me, fixing me for a second with its black eye. And in that moment, I suddenly feel her. It is like she is washing over me. Days later, as I type this paragraph, I glance out of the window and the robin is right there, at the back of the house this time, perched on a mossy stone, the sunlight warming its feathers. I think of the sparrow hawk I saw at a cousin's funeral earlier in the year, of the kestrel that swooped ahead of us as we walked Mum's coffin to the burial site. These birds are symbols of life rebirthed in a new form. I don't believe this robin *is* my mother, but I do feel she is inside it, around it, in the air that swirls as the mists descend from the hills and in the tumbling froth of the beck.

I think I am going to feel for the rest of my life that the world is a bit wrong, that there is always going to be what William Stafford describes as 'that form in the grass' – an imprint where something once was (in his poem, an antelope; in my life, my mother). But I will keep walking, swimming, writing, loving, learning to live alongside this shape of lack. As I spool back through Elisabeth's life, through memories of my mother, watching the stammering curve of my own life, I feel completely and fully what Pasternak meant when he wrote: 'You have always been in others and you will remain in others.' Perhaps that is what my mother meant when she said 'You are my Elisabeth.'

Elisabeth by a Canton waterfall

ACKNOWLEDGEMENTS

As I worked on this book I felt all along that I wasn't really writing it myself; that there were other hands guiding mine. Elisabeth's world has been a place of delight and escape, and I will miss her dearly. I hope she would approve of my telling of her story.

I would like to thank my agent Natalie Galustian for believing in the book, for her unstinting support and for providing me with fish pie at crucial moments. My editor Laura Barber has been sensitive, wise, attentive and encouraging at every turn. Working with her has been a huge honour. My thanks also go to the whole team at Granta, in particular to Daphne Tagg for her eagle-eyed copyediting, and Sarah Wasley and Christine Lo for seeing this safely from manuscript to book.

Early readers offered sage advice and invaluable suggestions. Thanks to Anna South, Juliette Mitchell, Beth Miller, Sarah Hawkins, Charles and Wiltrud Young, Tom Winnifrith, George and Aurelia Young, Kate Slater, Eleanor Knight, Alicia Meseguer Zafe, Tanya Shadrick, Sam Knowles, Derek Allen and Annie Mackey. Sorry to anyone I have missed off.

Love and gratitude to my brother and sister: thank you for being. I'm thankful to my father, stepmother, step- and half-siblings for their support and delight that this was going to be published. To my dear friends, profound thanks for your kindness and help. I couldn't have finished this book without you. My mother is the heart of this book and it would be wrong not to mention her here. Thank you, Mum, this was always for you.

Finally, my heartfelt thanks go to my beloved children, who have tolerated my writerly absences and immersion in the lives of others with a mixture of joyful enthusiasm and resigned stoicism, and to my amazing husband, without whom this and so many other things would not have been possible.

This is not a scholarly work, so I have not provided a full bibliography or notes. Much of my research draws directly on the diaries, letters and papers belonging to my family. I spent several happy days reading at the Mass Observation Archive at the University of Sussex, but I also cast my net far and wide for sources of information and inspiration. Particularly useful texts were Matt Cook's *A Gay History of Britain*, the work of Professor Louise Crewe, Ursula Buchan's *A Green and Pleasant Land* and Virginia Nicholson's *Millions Like Us*.

Those whose words I have directly quoted are listed below:
T. S. Eliot, *The Waste Land*; W.S. Merwin, 'Separation' from *Selected Poems* (Bloodaxe Books, 2007); William E. Stafford, *Ask Me* (edited by Kim Stafford); Captain Gordon Casserly, *The Land of the Boxers*; Albert Camus, *Notebooks 1951–1959* (trans.

Ryan Bloom); Alain de Botton, *Essays in Love*; Anaïs Nin, *The Diary of Anaïs Nin, Vol. 3. 1939–1944* (ed. Gunther Stuhlmann); Mildred Kemper Art Museum, *Eero Saarinen: Shaping the Future* (exhibition); Walter Isaacson, *Einstein: His Life and Universe*; Darwin Correspondence Project at the University of Cambridge; Rebecca Solnit, *A Field Guide to Getting Lost*; Joan Didion, *Slouching Towards Bethlehem*; Oliver Sacks' writings and ephemera found on www.brainpickings.org; Charles Baudelaire, 'Anywhere out of the World', *Poems in Prose* (trans. Arthur Symons); A. C. Grayling, *The Meaning of Things: Applying Philosophy to Life*; Susan Sontag, *As Consciousness is Harnessed to Flesh: Journals and Notebooks, 1964–1980*; Everett Ruess, *A Vagabond for Beauty* (ed. W. L. Rusho); Major S. Leigh Hunt, *Tropical Trials*; F. Scott Fitzgerald, *This Side of Paradise*; Olivia Laing, *The Lonely City*; Stephen Fry on Richard Herring's *Leicester Square Theatre Podcast*; Alice Oswald (introduction), *The Thunder Matters: 101 Poems for the Planet*; Jeanette Winterson, *Why Be Happy When You Can Be Normal?*; Jorge Louis Borges, 'Borges and I', in *The Maker*; Edgar Allan Poe, 'Tamerlane', *The Works of the Late Edgar Allan Poe*; Hilary Mantel, *Wolf Hall*; Blake Morrison, *And When Did You Last See Your Father?*; Cynthia Gladwyn, *The Paris Embassy*; Deborah Blum, *Love at Goon Park*; Katie Hickman, *Daughters of Britannia*; Henry James, *Letters Vol. 4* (ed. Percy Lubbock); Orson Wells, quoted in Neill Lochery, *Brazil*; Stefan Zweig, *Brazil: Land of the Future*; Edgard de Cerqueira Falcão, *Rio de Janeiro (Terras e Águas de Guanabara)*; Vladimir Nabokov, *Transparent Things*; Gaston Bachelard, *Water and Dreams*; Ted Hughes, *Letters of Ted Hughes* (ed. Christopher Reid); Virginia

Woolf, *Orlando*; Hilary Mantel on the *Culture Show*, BBC Two; John Donne, 'The Broken Heart', *The Poems of John Donne*; Boris Pasternak, *Doctor Zhivago*.